The Arthur Andersen Guide to
TALKING WITH YOUR CUSTOMERS

What They Will Tell You
about Your Business*

*When You Ask the Right Questions

Michael J. Wing

D1249502

ARTHUR
ANDERSEN

Upstart
Publishing Company
Specializing in Small Business Publishing
a division of Dearborn Publishing Group, Inc.

This book is dedicated to Pam, Lindsay, Jacque and Brody, without whose love and support this endeavor could not have been undertaken.

This publication is designed to provide accurate and authoritative information in regard to the subject matter covered. It is sold with the understanding that the publisher is not engaged in rendering legal, accounting, or other professional service. If legal advice or other expert assistance is required, the services of a competent professional person should be sought.

Executive Editor: Cynthia A. Zigmund
Managing Editor: Jack Kiburz
Interior Design: Lucy Jenkins
Cover Design: Salvatore Concialdi

Published by Upstart Publishing Company,
a division of Dearborn Publishing Group, Inc.

Printed in the United States of America

97 98 99 10 9 8 7 6 5 4 3 2

Library of Congress Cataloging-in-Publication Data

Wing, Michael J.
    The Arther Andersen guide to talking with your customers : what they will tell you about your business (when you ask the right questions) / Michael J. Wing, Arthur Andersen LLP.
        p. cm.
    Rev. ed. of : Talking with your customers. ©1993
    Includes index.
    ISBN 1-57410-075-0
    1. Customer relations.   2. Customer services.   3. Consumer satisfaction.   4. Motivation research (Marketing)   5. Market surveys.   I. Wing, Michael J.   Talking with your customers.
    II. Arthur Andersen LLP.   III. Title.
    HF5415.5.W6   1997
    658.8'12—dc21   97-7822
                                                          CIP

Upstart books are available at special quantity discounts to use as premiums and sales promotions, or for use in corporate training programs. For more information, please call the Special Sales Manager at 800-621-9621, ext. 4384, or write to Dearborn Financial Publishing, Inc., 155 N. Wacker Drive, Chicago, IL 60606-1719.

Foreword

The world is becoming increasingly competitive. Some have suggested that worldwide commerce is rapidly moving to commoditization, implying that virtually any product or service can be readily replaced by finding it elsewhere, whether domestically or internationally. The days of monopolistic enterprises are quickly fading into oblivion. Even utilities, long a bastion of monopolistic tendencies, will soon be in the midst of rigorous competition. As a result, the primary differentiating characteristic for companies is fast becoming the quality of service provided as perceived by the customer.

It's no longer enough to offer customers good products or services at competitive prices. It takes total customer satisfaction to keep customers and companies performing at their best. Achieving a superior level of satisfaction requires the uniting of two of the most powerful forces in business today: employees and customers.

Satisfied customers are loyal customers who purchase repeatedly from the company and recommend the company to others. In fact, we have found that repeat purchases from satisfied customers can account for up to 80 percent of company sales. Total customer satisfaction increases customer retention and employee satisfaction. The result can be a building of momentum that begins to drive up sales, drive down costs and increase profitability.

To respond to one another. To align service delivery processes with specific customer needs. To convert the short-term transaction into a long-term relationship. How does it start? With a course of action that is companywide, measurable and readily understandable.

This book is a very helpful tool to help you and your firm take that course of action. Mike Wing brings considerable experience from running four different firms. All were in highly competitive industries in which success turned on making customer satisfaction a competitive advantage. Wing has the experience of a practitioner in the field and brings his insights into focus in this book. The book is designed in a manner that is readily understandable. It is intended to help you turn insight into action. It is a book that we have personally found to be helpful and insightful and trust that you will as well. Best wishes for success as you seek to improve customer service in your company in order to maximize customer satisfaction and organizational performance.

Joseph P. O'Leary
Arthur Andersen
Chicago

Howard Barrett
Arthur Andersen
London

Acknowledgments

The author wishes to acknowledge the tremendous assistance provided by Patrick Hogan throughout the conception and editing process; the long hours contributed by Rod Woodard in typing the manuscript; and the encouragement of many "customers" desirous of such a book.

Contents

Preface

All businesses need programs in place that will allow them to regularly "talk" with their customers. There is no better or more efficient way to know how your firm is doing or how your products, services and employees are perceived in the marketplace than by asking your customers.

The cost of not talking with your customers can be staggering. On average, two-thirds of customers that leave a firm to do business with another do so because of perceived indifferent attitudes of the owner, manager or employees. Only 4 percent of dissatisfied customers will take the time to complain to the firm; the vast majority leave quietly to share their dissatisfaction within their spheres of influence.

Ironically, the average firm in America spends six times more money on efforts to attract new customers than it does on efforts designed to nurture and keep its existing customers. It is up to you to ask your customers on a regular basis how you are doing, how you can serve them better, what they perceive are your strengths and weaknesses, and who they regard as your competition and why. The goal of "talking" with your customers is for you to formulate a strategy for keeping your hard-earned customers.

During the early part of my career, I became increasingly frustrated with the lack of effective resources for measuring and managing customer satisfaction. As a result, I developed high quality customized instruments for just such a purpose. This led to the derivation of customized instruments for conducting widespread customer satisfaction assessments across hundreds of different industries. As a senior manager with Arthur Andersen, I design customer satisfaction assessments, conduct comprehensive analyses and provide other management-related services. Over the years I have worked with a broad spectrum of businesses and associations, both domestic and international. I have seen firsthand the problems caused by poor customer service as well as the amazing results superior customer service can produce.

Few books available on customer service contain the hands-on advice that you will find in this book. I have included numerous worksheets and time-tested surveys, including the following:

- Self-assessment surveys that will ensure an ongoing evaluation of your customer-service performance
- Sample surveys that can serve as models for your own efforts
- Sample letters covering a variety of situations that may impact customer service

In *The Arthur Andersen Guide to Talking with Your Customers*, I have provided the tools that will help you make customer satisfaction an integral component of your business strategy. Asking the right questions will yield information that is useful in every aspect of your business—marketing, finance, employee management and the sales process, to name a few.

Small businesses have traditionally focused on customer service as a competitive advantage. Lacking the bureaucratic layers of management of larger corporations, small companies often have the flexibility to be more responsive to their customers. However, the same customer-service concepts and tools are available to an organization of any size, whether in the public or private sector.

In today's competitive economy, large businesses are placing more resources in formal customer-service programs. Small businesses must be prepared to meet the challenge. The resources available to small businesses are limited, and these companies can ill-afford to spend their time, money and energy in efforts not clearly focused on their customers' needs.

Providing superior customer service and creating customer satisfaction will continue to be the crucial elements in determining which organizations will "win" and which will "lose." It is my sincere hope that this book will help move your business into the "win" column.

1

How Do You Know How You're Doing Unless You Ask?

Sam represents the third generation involved in running the family-owned business—a specialty toy store located in a large midwestern city. When asked how he knows how well the store is doing with respect to its customers, Sam wryly replies, "I have been in or around this store for most of my 60 years. I've seen a lot of kids grow up and bring their kids into the store. I know my customers all too well."

When pressed, Sam acknowledges that revenues for the store have been flat over the past several years. Reluctantly, he agrees to conduct a customer satisfaction assessment. What he finds is enlightening: Customers like his store for tradition's sake but purchase most of their toys elsewhere because of competitive prices; the demographics of his primary customer base have changed dramatically; and the hours of operation and promotions offered are largely ineffective.

Upon receiving this information and suggestions for improvement, Sam makes some modifications. Within months, the store's monthly revenues as well as profits increase.

Sam is quoted as saying that he only wishes he asked customers how the store was doing earlier—he plans on asking on a regular basis from now on.

Customer satisfaction is one of those topics that everyone claims to know something about: from the company executive who just announced a comprehensive customer-service program, to the employee in receipt of the latest management customer initiative, to the customer who beats a path to the service provider that has an excellent product or service at a reasonable price, and treats him or her in an important manner. Many customers are growing weary of the search for such organizations.

In his book *The Marketing Imagination,* Theodore Levitt describes the importance of paying attention to your customers.

> The natural tendencies of relationships, whether in marriage or in business, is entropy, meaning the erosion or deterioration of sensitivity and attentiveness. A healthy relationship maintains, and preferably expands, the equity and the possibilities that were created during courtship. A healthy relationship requires a conscious and constant fight against the forces of entropy. It becomes important for the business person to regularly and seriously ask, "How are we doing?" "Is the relationship improving or deteriorating?" "Are we neglecting anything?"

The irony associated with customer satisfaction in today's economy is profound. No business intentionally decides to do a bad job, few ever say, "We don't believe in customer service. We try to do a poor job. We are going to go out today, lose customers and make them dissatisfied." Quite the contrary, if asked, most would probably indicate that they or their company are trying to please customers to the best of their ability.

Quality Service Is a Competitive Necessity

The impact of customer dissatisfaction can be staggering. For example, if an organization were able to handle 99.9 percent of transactions accurately, there might still be plenty of room for error. Consider the following:

- 99.9 percent of accurate transactions might be 22,000 checks deducted from an incorrect account every hour.

- 99.9 percent of accurate handling might mean the U.S. Postal Service loses more than 17,000 pieces of mail every hour.

- 99.9 percent accuracy might mean more than 3,700 incorrectly filled prescriptions each day.

The purpose of an enterprise is to gain and keep customers. It is self-evident that without customers in sufficient and steady numbers, there is no business. And no business can function effectively without a clear view of what prospective customers want. An understanding of competition, perception, product, pricing and relevance of strategies and programs may enable a business to keep its customers but the key is customer service. Whether you are buried in research and development, in the executive suite, in shipping or at the switchboard, customer service is everyone's responsibility.

Clear and usable information is essential to accurately track customer satisfaction. Such information is an integral part of monitoring performance and validating, or invalidating, key marketing assumptions of the business.

Large firms usually have had more experience with research endeavors than smaller ones. Many forces come into play here: resources and staff availability, experience and sophistication are a few. Many times such firms also are saddled with bureaucracy, inertia and turf battles, all of which serve to impede responsiveness. It can be like trying to quickly move an aircraft carrier.

The Small Business Perspective

Smaller companies, on the other hand, are often faced with the "tyranny of the urgent" because of limited resources, few employees and little experience with research. Many of these small to medium-sized organizations are heavily collateralized or have borrowed from family or friends. These businesspeople usually are characterized by a tremendous work ethic and a great desire to succeed. And, many times, decisions are based on intuition, gut feeling, a recently read article, a recently attended trade show or the axiom "that's the way we've always done it." Virtually no ongoing, systematic, statistically valid customer satisfaction measurement process exists in these organizations. However, small businesses can and should conduct regular assessments of customer satisfaction. Imagine, if you will then, that the segment of the economy that is creating the most jobs is often the least equipped in terms of information to make the best decisions concerning its future.

The Customer Component

How does your organization know how it's doing? For most, the response would be quantitatively based. For example:

- This month we're ahead of last month (or the converse).
- This quarter we're ahead of last quarter (or the converse).
- Budget versus actual
- This year versus last year
- Region A versus Region B
- Product X versus Product Y

The profit and loss statement (and other quantitative measures) is certainly a very important tool; that is not disputed. With the proliferation of computers, most businesses have access to information; in fact, some argue too much information. Many managers are busy calculating and comparing figures for this month versus last month, this quarter versus last quarter, this year versus last year, today versus the same day last year; all of which is very important information. These measures allow the manager to weigh why the company is above or below forecasts and what corrective actions can be taken.

However, what is noticeably absent from this enormous amount of data is input from the customer. Where is a customer's perspective in the three-inch-thick sales report, shipping log or income statement? What does the *customer* think about the operation? By the time a problem with a customer is reflected in an income statement, the customer has already taken his or her business elsewhere. The income statement, by definition, is a historical document! The customers have gone elsewhere. Consequently, more sales meetings are called, advertising is changed, and there are more programs and promotional campaigns. "We've got to do something to get sales up!" becomes the battle cry.

Although well-intentioned, most of the time these actions are knee-jerk responses. The company usually doesn't know why customers left or where they went. By the time their migration is reflected by lost revenue on the income statement, it is too late; the customers are gone.

When presented with such a scenario, some executives insist that their company is different. For example, one executive said, "When customers complain to us, we bury them with kindness. The vice-president takes them to lunch, and if it is a really important customer, the president will take them to lunch, and follow up with a letter. Our customer-service representatives will call them and, if necessary, will offer a discount and extended terms. We'll win them back!"

This attitude is commendable, but on average, only 4 percent of dissatisfied customers take time to complain. Thus, although a company may have a program for winning back dissatisfied customers, it may be reaching only the 4 percent who complain. Ninety-six percent of dissatisfied customers go away quietly but become very vocal in their respective spheres of influence. The average dissatisfied customer will tell eight to ten people about their unsatisfactory experience. They'll complain to friends, associates and people at church, social clubs, country clubs, etc.

Migration is a serious financial blow to those who don't know how to measure and manage customer satisfaction. And it is an extraordinary opportunity for those who do.

Customer-Service Checkup

All businesses should undergo a regular customer-service checkup and should know how they are perceived by their customers. As individuals, we've grown accustomed to checking our pulse after exercising and to the importance of periodic checkups. Most people would think it unwise to go for an extended period of time without a physical. This should also apply to a business.

There are several different means by which a customer-service checkup can be accomplished. Some of the more common methods are personal interviews, focus groups, telephone surveys, mall intercepts and mailed questionnaires. The strengths and weaknesses of these methods will be discussed in greater detail in Chapter 3.

For such research to be successful, it should be clear and understandable. There are many executives that have nicely bound reports in their offices with research dated 1993, 1994, 1995, 1996, etc. But when asked what valuable information was gleaned from such documents, they often admit that they are unsure, that it was a process followed for years by their predecessor or they were uncomfortable with statistics in school.

Quality Service Is an Ongoing Project

Providing quality service requires that a business be vigilant in its awareness of its efforts and performance. To aid in that process, I have included assessments at the end of each chapter. The assessments provide an opportunity for you to objectively evaluate your company's efforts against a standard. It is recommended that you complete the assessments immediately after reading each chapter. Then, establish a timetable within which subsequent assessments of company efforts will be conducted. Keep completed assessments on file for comparative purposes.

That is not to suggest that your company's efforts may not be exemplary, but rather that it is always wise to have your efforts objectively affirmed. For maximum use of the assessments, carefully review and customize them to apply to your company's specific set of circumstances.

Notes on Using the Assessment

The assessment exercise is not intended to be all-inclusive; each organization and the market in which it operates is unique. The questions raised are intended to help an organization go beyond the facade of "rationalizing" its action or inaction. The assessment tools provided herein are intended to be insightful. It is important that each organization determine the specific relevance of the assessment with respect to its specific situation.

Scoring the Assessment

Filling Out the Form

1. If the statement is generally true of your organization, mark the "yes" column.
2. If the statement is not true of your organization, mark the "no" column.
3. If the statement is occasionally true of your organization, mark the "sometimes" column.
4. If a particular statement does not have relevance to your organization or if information is not available for a credible response, then draw a line through the statement.

Evaluating the Responses

1. A negative answer is seldom favorable. It indicates an absence of a particular activity that may or may not be compensated for elsewhere.
2. A positive answer is almost always favorable. However, too many "yes" answers may indicate that your response is not sufficiently objective.
3. Several "sometimes" answers may point to a lack of direction or commitment.
4. Several "crossed off" questions may indicate insufficient records or an inadequate data base.

Rating the Responses

1. Upon completion of the assessment form, award points as follows:
    - For each "yes" answer, award one point.
    - For each "sometimes" answer, award one-half point.
    - For each "no" answer, award zero points.
    - For each question crossed off the list, award zero points, and deduct one from the total number of questions in the assessment.
2. Divide the total number of points awarded by the number of questions on the assessment (less the number of questions crossed off the list).

$$\text{Score} = \frac{\text{Number of points awarded}}{\text{Number of questions answered}}$$

A score of 1 is excellent. Scores less than 1 should be evaluated with respect to their distance from 1. The farther the score is from 1, the more removed the organization is from initiating actions that are beneficial to superior customer service.

Introductory Organizational Assessment of Customer-Service Activities

Organization: _____   Date: _____   Person Conducting Assessment: _____

		Yes	No	Sometimes
1.	Procedures are in place for handling customer problems and complaints.	_____	_____	_____
2.	All personnel who communicate directly with customers— whether in person, by telephone or in writing—are trained in proper conduct and attitude.	_____	_____	_____
3.	The actions of personnel who communicate with customers are guided by written procedures and standard practices.	_____	_____	_____
4.	Personnel who communicate directly with customers regularly meet with supervisors to discuss customer concerns and complaints.	_____	_____	_____
5.	The handling of customer complaints is audited on a regular basis to confirm the proper resolution of problems, adherence to standard procedures, and to determine if a change in procedure is required.	_____	_____	_____
6.	Information on the availability of products and services is issued to personnel regularly.	_____	_____	_____
7.	Individual managers are held responsible for the loss of customers and/or cancellation of orders resulting from inadequate customer service.	_____	_____	_____

Page total: _____ + _____ + _____ = ☐

	Yes	No	Sometimes
8. A complaint/concern log is kept, showing the nature and source of problems and complaints as well as the steps taken to solve them.	———	———	———
9. Complaint/concern logs are regularly reviewed by management to improve performance in customer service and to correct deficiencies in services and products.	———	———	———
10. Customers are frequently asked to evaluate the firm's customer service and offer suggestions for improvement.	———	———	———
11. Employees are frequently asked to evaluate the firm's customer-service efforts and offer suggestions for improvement.	———	———	———
12. There is an active, ongoing effort to improve the quality and accuracy of communication with the customer (e.g., accelerating response time, eliminating billing errors, providing better technical assistance and establishing clear and consistent customer relation policies).	———	———	———
13. Efforts are made on a regular basis to determine how field personnel are doing in serving customer needs.	———	———	———
14. The order processing procedures have been reviewed in the past year to assess how the process can be made more convenient for customers.	———	———	———
15. The effectiveness of the order processing function is evaluated periodically.	———	———	———

Page total:

——— + ——— + ——— = ☐

	Yes	No	Sometimes
16. Postsale service and support is recognized as an essential activity that has top management support and is deemed as an integral component to meeting customer needs and achieving success.	——————	——————	——————
17. The organization regularly obtains valid statistical data pertaining to how customers and prospective customers view its services and/or products.	——————	——————	——————
18. Individual departments are staffed with trained customer-service personnel who are well informed about the organization's products, services, policies and customers.	——————	——————	——————
19. All new employees are given formal customer-service training before serving in frontline customer contact positions.	——————	——————	——————
20. The effectiveness of postsale service and support is periodically evaluated by comparing actual performance to established benchmarks.	——————	——————	——————
21. If employees provide superior customer service, they are compensated accordingly.	——————	——————	——————
22. Good communication exists among departments so that service challenges are resolved with minimum inconvenience to the customer.	——————	——————	——————
23. All employees have the attitude that the customer comes first.	——————	——————	——————

Page total: —————— + —————— + —————— = ☐

Page 1 Total: =   ☐

Page 2 Total: =   ☐

Page 3 Total: =   ☐

Exercise Total: =   ☐

2

What Are Your Customers' Expectations?

A medium-sized professional association located in the Northeast with a national membership base has experienced a steady, incremental increase in its membership over several years.

However, a series of proposed legislative initiatives in different parts of the country perceived to be detrimental to the profession have swelled the membership ranks over a 12-month period.

Even though the association endeavors to provide the same type and quality of service to its membership that it has in previous years, it is unable to do so in many areas.

Growing increasingly frustrated, association management commissions an assessment of its membership base to determine its expectations in different areas. It has not conducted such an assessment before.

The study finds that in one area where the association is seeking to ship publications within 48 hours, members stated that the receipt of such materials within three to four weeks is very acceptable. However, members expect the phones to be answered promptly and inquiries to be addressed accurately and efficiently.

With such information, the association is able to modify its service level in direct response to member expectations—the end result being an increase in member satisfaction and a reduction in cost, even though the membership base has increased.

P roviding a product or service your customers perceive as excellent requires you to know what it is that your customers expect. This is the most critical component of delivering excellent customer service.

Virtually every company thinks it knows what its customers want. However, if your company is only slightly inaccurate about its assumptions, you could lose your customers' business to another company that has more accurately filled their needs.

Being only "slightly" inaccurate can lead your organization to spend money, time and effort on things that are not important to your customers. And in a worst-case scenario, it can mean not surviving in an intensely competitive environment.

The Expectation Gap

There are times when a gap occurs between what customers expect and what management presumes they expect. This often happens because companies overlook or don't fully understand customers' perceptions and expectations. In spite of a strong commitment and sincere desire to provide quality service, many companies fall dramatically short of the mark, usually because they have an internally directed rather than externally directed focus. An internally directed focus assumes that the company knows what customers *should* want and delivers or produces that. This orientation often leads to providing products and services that do not match customers' expectations—important features and benefits may be left out and levels of performance may be inadequate.

In looking at several different types of organizations, there are common elements that contribute to the gap between customer expectations and the product or service offered. The common elements are as follows:

- Inadequate "bilateral" communication between frontline personnel and management
- An absence of regular interaction between management and customers
- An absence of a strong marketing-research program
- An absence of customer-service accountability

Communicating with Frontline Employees

Frontline employees are in regular contact with customers. As a result, they know a great deal about customers' perceptions and expectations. This information must be regularly passed on to management. When these channels of communication are closed or inadequate, management lacks key feedback about problems occurring in product and service delivery as well as critical information about changing customer expectations.

Communication between frontline employees and management can be enhanced in a number of ways. Some of the more common methods are as follows:

- Formal types of communication (e.g., memos, suggestion cards, open meetings)
- Informal communication (e.g., discussions over coffee, walking around the facility, going out into the field)

While it is critically important to assess customers' perceptions and expectations regularly, it is also very important to assess whether management understands the needs and expectations of frontline employees. Management that communicates with frontline people not only builds morale but also learns a tremendous amount about their customers, thereby reducing the expectation gap.

Here are some questions to ask concerning the communication between management and frontline employees in your organization:

- How often do managers have direct contact with frontline employees?
- Do managers encourage suggestions from frontline employees concerning the quality of your product or service?
- Are there too many levels of management, causing managers to be cut off from direct contact with and feedback from frontline employees?
- Are there formal or informal opportunities for frontline employees to communicate with management on a regular basis?
- Has management adequately determined and monitored the expectations of frontline employees?
- Do frontline employees feel strongly supported?

Interaction Between Management and Customers

The larger a company is, the more difficult it is for managers to deal directly with customers. Consequently, managers have less information about customers' perceptions and expectations. However, with smaller companies, managers can receive more direct information concerning their customers.

Even when they are regularly provided with reports, managers readily lose the customer perspective if they don't have the opportunity for direct customer contact. Theoretical knowledge is a poor substitute for a face-to-face encounter.

To truly understand and appreciate customers' needs and expectations, managers should experience first-hand what really happens in the field, in stores, or when answering the customer-service line, working the service line or dealing with customers face-to-face. Managers can better empathize with employees if they have experienced some of what employees deal with on a regular basis. Here are some questions to consider concerning regular interaction between management and customers:

- Is there a program in place in your company where managers rotate to different service positions within the organization?

- Does top management make it a priority to get out in the field and see customers?

- Do managers randomly interact with customers (i.e., those waiting in line, browsing in the store or calling the service desk)?

The Need for a Strong Marketing Program

Since marketing research is a vitally important tool in assessing customers' perceptions and expectations, a company that does not regularly collect such information may be more likely to have a significant customer expectation gap. A company that does some marketing research, but not in the area of customer perceptions and expectations, may also be producing a significant gap.

To effectively deal with expectation versus performance issues, marketing research measurements should focus on product or service quality issues, such as which features and benefits are most important to customers; how much do customers expect, at what price and in what time frame; and what do customers think the company should do if problems occur in product or service delivery. Determining what your customers expect is absolutely essential to providing superior quality.

Regardless of your company's size and resources, there are means by which such marketing research activity can take place. Several different methodologies are summarized in Chapter 3.

Questions to consider concerning your company's marketing research efforts are as follows:

- Is research conducted on a regular basis to generate high-quality, reliable information about what your customers want and expect?

- Does your research focus on quality of service provided?

- Can research findings be readily understood and utilized by your managers?

- Are the research findings an integral component of planning the company's strategic directions?

- Are research findings shared throughout the company when appropriate?

Customer-Service Accountability

Policies and procedures are important, but when they impede a firm's ability to meet customer needs, they are counterproductive. With many companies experiencing an increase in policies and procedures over the last several years, initiative has been stifled and employees are less willing to get involved.

For companies to compete effectively in an increasingly competitive marketplace, employees must be empowered to identify problems, resolve them and share suggestions with management. It is detrimental for employees to withdraw into a bureaucratized environment and assume that someone else will take care of the problems. All the while, customers may be migrating elsewhere.

The following are questions to ask regarding customer-service accountability within your business:

- Are employees encouraged to "take ownership" of a problem, and are they supported in their efforts?

- Is your business unduly bureaucratized, and does it encourage an attitude of "someone else will take care of it"?
- Does your business empower its employees to find ways in which customers can be better served?

If the actions described in this chapter, are taken by an organization, regardless of size, it will greatly facilitate management's knowledge of customers' expectations and will enable the organization to move effectively to close expectation gaps.

The expectation scorecard in Figure 2.1 will help you determine where expectation gaps may presently exist. Figure 2.2 is a flowchart that shows potential expectation pitfalls and actions required.

FIGURE 2.1 Customer Expectations Scorecard

Instructions for Use of Scorecard

It is necessary to use survey information in conjunction with this scorecard. Values are as follows:

(A)   These values refer to how a business scored in the survey in each category. The average performance score in the aggregate is used.

(B)   These values refer to what customers expect in each category. The average expectation score in the aggregate is used.

(C)   This value is a ratio of (A) over (B).

(A) Performance Score	Categories (for reference only)	(B) Customer Expectation Score	(C) Customer Satisfaction Ratio (A/B)
_____	Shipping	_____	_____
_____	Product quality	_____	_____
_____	Price	_____	_____
_____	Phone service	_____	_____
_____	Sales force knowledge	_____	_____
_____	Frequency of contact by sales force	_____	_____
_____	Professionalism of staff	_____	_____
_____	Expertise	_____	_____
_____	Problems handled effectively	_____	_____
_____	Responsiveness	_____	_____
_____	Understanding customer needs	_____	_____
_____	Accessibility of personnel	_____	_____
_____	Reliability of products	_____	_____

$$\text{Customer satisfaction ratio} = \frac{\text{Performance}}{\text{Customer expectation}}$$

The desired objective is a customer satisfaction ratio greater than one in each category and as an overall score.

FIGURE 2.2   Customer versus Business Expectation Pitfalls

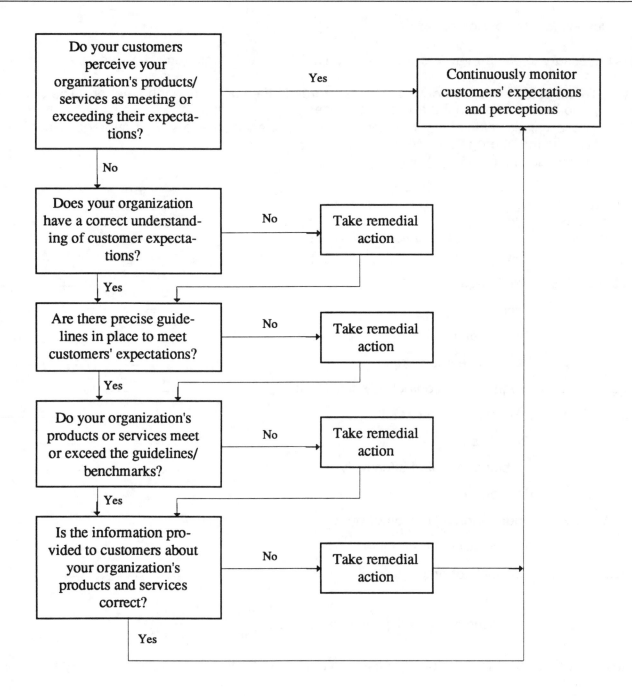

Notes on Using the Assessment

The assessment exercise is not intended to be all-inclusive; each organization and the market in which it operates is unique. The questions raised are intended to help an organization go beyond the facade of "rationalizing" its action or inaction. The assessment tools provided herein are intended to be insightful. It is important that each organization determine the specific relevance of the assessment with respect to its specific situation.

Scoring the Assessment

Filling Out the Form

1. If the statement is generally true of your organization, mark the "yes" column.
2. If the statement is not true of your organization, mark the "no" column.
3. If the statement is occasionally true of your organization, mark the "sometimes" column.
4. If a particular statement does not have relevance to your organization or if information is not available for a credible response, then draw a line through the statement.

Evaluating the Responses

1. A negative answer is seldom favorable. It indicates an absence of a particular activity that may or may not be compensated for elsewhere.
2. A positive answer is almost always favorable. However, too many "yes" answers may indicate that your response is not sufficiently objective.
3. Several "sometimes" answers may point to a lack of direction or commitment.
4. Several "crossed off" questions may indicate insufficient records or an inadequate data base.

Rating the Responses

1. Upon completion of the assessment form, award points as follows:
    - For each "yes" answer, award one point.
    - For each "sometimes" answer, award one-half point.
    - For each "no" answer, award zero points.
    - For each question crossed off the list, award zero points, and deduct one from the total number of questions in the assessment.
2. Divide the total number of points awarded by the number of questions on the assessment (less the number of questions crossed off the list).

$$\text{Score} = \frac{\text{Number of points awarded}}{\text{Number of questions answered}}$$

A score of 1 is excellent. Scores less than 1 should be evaluated with respect to their distance from 1. The farther the score is from 1, the more removed the organization is from initiating actions that are beneficial to superior customer service.

Handling Customer Expectations and Perceptions

Organization: _____   Date: _____   Person Conducting Assessment: _____

	Yes	No	Sometimes
1. The organization seeks to regularly identify the expectations and perceptions of customers.	_____	_____	_____
2. The organization regularly evaluates how well its products or services are meeting customer expectations and perceptions.	_____	_____	_____
3. The organization implements standards of performance in providing its products or services to customers.	_____	_____	_____
4. The organization regularly reviews product and service claims to make sure they are consistent with what is being delivered.	_____	_____	_____
5. The organization uses customer complaints to strategically identify problem areas.	_____	_____	_____
6. The organization regularly studies its competitors to determine other expectations and perceptions.	_____	_____	_____
7. The organization regularly conducts research on direct and intermediate customers to gain in-depth information about expectations.	_____	_____	_____
8. The organization regularly conducts studies on key customers to gain in-depth information concerning expectations.	_____	_____	_____

Page total: _____ + _____ + _____ = ☐

	Yes	No	Sometimes

9. The organization holds customer meetings to provide a continuous source of information on customers' changing expectations.

   ———   ———   ———

10. The organization conducts studies on various transactions to provide feedback on the quality of service provided at different stages.

   ———   ———   ———

11. The organization actively seeks to reduce the number of layers between management and the customer.

   ———   ———   ———

12. The organization actively increases the amount of contact and communication between management and frontline employees.

   ———   ———   ———

13. The organization actively seeks to standardize tasks.

   ———   ———   ———

14. The organization has clearly defined goals for individual employees and grants them responsibility to make decisions.

   ———   ———   ———

15. The organization provides adequate resources and supervision to enable employees to perform assigned customer-service tasks.

   ———   ———   ———

16. The organization implements periodic job reviews to determine if employees are performing well. If not, changes are instituted so that customer needs are appropriately met.

   ———   ———   ———

17. The organization gives employees the freedom to make decisions to satisfy customers' needs.

   ———   ———   ———

18. The organization encourages employees to learn new ways to better serve customers.

   ———   ———   ———

Page total: ——— **+** ——— **+** ——— **=** ☐

	Yes	No	Sometimes
19. The organization strives to make sure that customers and managers have the same expectations of employees.	——	——	——
20. The organization produces policies and procedures for serving customers that are consistent throughout the organization.	——	——	——
21. The organization briefs frontline employees about forthcoming external communications before they occur.	——	——	——
22. The organization facilitates interaction between frontline employees and the sales department to discuss the level of service provided to customers.	——	——	——
23. The organization provides frontline employees the opportunity to review advertising before it occurs.	——	——	——
24. The organization's management communicates goals and expectations to employees.	——	——	——

Page total: —— + —— + —— = ☐

Page 1 Total: = ☐

Page 2 Total: = ☐

Page 3 Total: = ☐

Exercise Total: = ☐

3

What Do You Want To Know?

A small retailer in the Midwest has, by its own admission, "gone through the motions" in measuring customer satisfaction over the last few years. Its efforts have largely consisted of a blank card by the cash register that says, "How are we doing?" The occasional responses received are largely nondescript.

Alice, the proprietor, faced with increasing competition, determines that if such activity is to continue, it must provide specific useful information: Who is the perceived competition? What are the store's distinctive strengths? What customer needs are not being met?

The instrument she chooses provides excellent information pertaining to the store's relative strengths and weaknesses, specific suggestions for improvement and valuable price and product insight.

Empowered with such information on a regular basis, Alice not only competes favorably but has carved out a position of market dominance.

In *Thriving on Chaos* Tom Peters coins the term *engaged listening.* This means giving your organization sufficient opportunities to assess customers' ideas and experiences and then squeezing the last drop of potential from every encounter with a customer who has something he or she believes is important for you to hear.

For purposes of this book, *listening* and *measuring* shall be treated as synonymous terms. The goal here is to transform listening into a more formal process and to treat it as an integral component of your business.

In organizations of every kind, size and description, an important priority today is to listen to customers, try to understand what it is they are saying and then formulate an effective course of action. According to Peters, "Listening to customers must become everyone's business. With most competitors moving ever faster, the race will go to those who listen and respond most intently."

Purposeful Listening

Listening must have a purpose. There are five main reasons why a business should measure customer satisfaction:

1.   To understand the various "moments of truth" customers encounter and what these experiences are like.

2.   To keep current on market developments—the sum of customers' wants, needs and expectations. In an era of constant change, customer needs and expectations will be fluid as well.

3.   To identify new trends (positive or negative) and possibly uncover unexpected ideas or opportunities much earlier in the process.

4.   Seriously listening to customers is an excellent way to involve them in your business. The customers may think that the company cares enough to ask or is trying to serve them better. This is more likely to encourage them to respond with information that is of significant benefit to the company.

5.   The business truly wants to know how satisfied its customers are. It wants to determine what customers say and perceive about the firm and is willing to act upon this information.

Setting Objectives

Prior to initiating your company's listening efforts, ask yourself what is the purpose behind the initiative. There must be a clear set of objectives as to what is to be measured in the process. What are your company's objectives in determining levels of satisfaction? For example, it may have several different constituencies to work with and may need to respond to each of them in different ways. Which customers are especially important? Your company may offer several kinds of services or products. Which ones do you want to evaluate? Over what period of time? The mix of customers, services or products targeted for evaluation can be all-inclusive or not. However, the mix selected will be as unique as the service or product you provide. If listening to customers is to be productive and not simply just an activity you must decide to whom you are going to listen, when, where and what you are listening for. This will help you determine how you can best acquire information. In contemplating your objectives, review what you plan to do with the information once received. Ask yourself the following questions:

- Will the information be used to form a marketing plan?
- Will the information be used to assess marketing efforts?
- Will it be used to identify competition?
- Will it be used to evaluate awareness and utilization of products or services?
- Will it identify strengths or weaknesses?
- Will it be used to assess customer perceptions and determine levels of customer satisfaction?

The list of questions can grow to be very extensive. Consequently, taking time to evaluate the purpose of your inquiry carefully and including employees and other relevant staff is time well spent. (An objectives worksheet is provided in Figure 3.1.)

Unfortunately, there are far too many organizations today that have reams of information but have not found a use for the information or the means of assessing it. It is dangerous to try to measure too much in one survey, as the respondents may be overwhelmed and may grow fatigued—the organization may be trying to measure too wide a subject matter. As a consequence, the quality of information can suffer and the value of the exercise can be significantly reduced. It is better to measure fewer things well than too many things poorly.

Someone once said, "Listening is half a loaf. Doing something with what you learn feeds the multitude." Thus, determining your company's objectives prior to commencing a listening program is critical so that the information proves useful. An overview of a research design process that begins with the setting of objectives can be found in Figure 3.2. Sample questionnaires are shown in Figures 3.3 and 3.4, and a sample response letter to customers is provided in Figure 3.5.

The chapters that follow show how information that is effectively collected from customers can prove invaluable in helping to maximize a company's performance.

FIGURE 3.1 Objectives Worksheet

This worksheet is not designed to be all-inclusive. It is intended to help you determine your assessment objectives.

Marketing

- ❑ Market share
- ❑ Competition—who and why
- ❑ Promotion and advertising efforts
- ❑ Awareness of firm
- ❑ Awareness of products or services offered
- ❑ Location
- ❑ Strengths and weaknesses
- ❑ Price versus value relationship
- ❑ Price versus quantity relationship
- ❑ New product or service suggestions
- ❑ Demographics

Organization

- ❑ Professionalism
- ❑ Frequency of contact
- ❑ Courtesy
- ❑ Competence
- ❑ Attitude
- ❑ Quality of staff
- ❑ Returning phone calls
- ❑ Location
- ❑ Problem-solving skills
- ❑ Efficiency

Finance

- ❑ Price sensitivity
- ❑ Utilization of different products or services
- ❑ Facility assessment
- ❑ External appearance
- ❑ Allocation of capital resources
- ❑ Return on assets

FIGURE 3.2   Research Design Process Steps

Step	Description
1. Define the research project objective.	Clearly specify the information required and the scope of the target.
2. Select the data collection method.	Determine whether questionnaires, phone surveys, focus groups, etc., will be the best method of collection.
3. Select the method of measurement.	Determine how the information should be received for best utilization. If necessary, go back to step 2 to pick an alternative method that is more consistent with the analytical tools available.
4. Select the sample.	Determine who and how many respondents to measure.
5. Begin designing the survey.	Design the size and format of the survey while adhering to generally accepted statistical principles.
6. Specify the time frame for the project and the estimated financial cost.	Determine the date by which the completed information is required and then solve backwards, providing costs for each step.
7. Prepare a summation document.	Summarize the key components of the preceding steps so that the appropriate employees are properly informed prior to beginning the project.
8. Provide regular updates to company participants.	Provide a weekly, biweekly or monthly timetable to company participants so they are informed as to the progress made (e.g., response rate, etc.).
9. Present formal findings.	Present the final report in a manner consistent with the data format requested in Step 3.
10. Formulate an action plan based on findings, and communicate relevant findings to the target sample.	The action plan allows information to have an immediate impact—both internally and externally.

FIGURE 3.3   Sample Questionnaire #1

Company Description   The company that used the following questionnaire is a quality food distributor. Components of its product line are sent to different parts of the country.

Objectives   The objectives of the customer assessment included the following:

- Obtain profile of customers.

- Assess performance of company.

- Assess performance of company vis-à-vis competition.

- Determine percentage of customer purchases from your company (as opposed to others in your field).

- Identify future trends.

- Identify perceived strengths and weaknesses.

- Solicit suggestions for improvement.

XYZ FOODS, INC.

Rocky Mountain, Colorado

Dear Valued Customer,

Our success at XYZ Foods, Inc., is built around our ability to meet the needs of our customers. Like any other business, we must constantly ask ourselves, "How are we doing?"

Often the best approach is to let our customers answer that question for us. By taking a few moments to complete this customer survey, you will help us evaluate our performance.

We have asked Any Research Firm, Inc.—an independent marketing-research firm—to conduct this survey on our behalf. Their expert analysis will give us an accurate, objective reading of our strengths and weaknesses.

Your responses will be kept completely confidential. We have enclosed a postage-paid envelope for your convenience.

We appreciate your willingness to assist us. Thank you for taking the time to respond to our questions. We'll be listening.

Sincerely,

Joan Doe
President

1234 Any Street • Topeka, KS 66000 • Telephone: (913) 555-1212 Fax: (913) 555-1234

Questionnaire

1. What type of company do you represent? _____
   - ❏ Full-line distributor
   - ❏ Processor
   - ❏ Meat/poultry/seafood distributor
   - ❏ Chain restaurant
   - ❏ Chain supermarket
   - ❏ Independent grocer
   - ❏ Stir-fry market
   - ❏ Other:_____

2. In what state is your firm located? _____ (Please provide the two-letter state abbreviation.)

3. What approximately, is your annual sales revenue?
   - ❏ Less than $100,000
   - ❏ $100,000 to $500,000
   - ❏ $500,01 to $1,000,000
   - ❏ $1,000,001 to $5,000,000
   - ❏ $5,000,001 to $25,000,000
   - ❏ Over $25,000,000

4. Do you pick up your orders from XYZ Foods, or are they delivered?
   - ❏ Pickup
   - ❏ Delivered (Please answer 4a.)
     - 4a. If delivered, are your orders shipped?
       - ❏ Prepaid
       - ❏ Collect
       - ❏ Don't know

5. Do you purchase from suppliers other than XYZ Foods?
   - ❏ Yes (Answer 5a, 5b, 5c.)
   - ❏ No
     - 5a. If yes, from whom do you purchase? _____

5b. If yes, why do you buy from other suppliers? _____

_____

5c. If yes, how do other suppliers market their products to you?
   ❏ By telephone   ❏ By mail   ❏ By personal visits

6. What percentage of your stir-fry purchases are XYZ Foods?_____
   ❏ Less than 10%   ❏ 10 to 25%   ❏ 26 to 50%   ❏ 51 to 75%   ❏ Over 75%

7. Whom do you perceive to be XYZ Foods' primary competitors? _____

_____

Why? _____

_____

8. Have you purchased from XYZ Foods in the past three months?
   ❏ Yes   ❏ No (Answer 8a.)
   8a. If no, why not? _____

_____

9. Are you aware that XYZ Foods sells fresh rice?
   ❏ Yes (Answer 9a.)   ❏ No
   9a. If yes, do you buy fresh rice from XYZ Foods?
      ❏ Yes   ❏ No (Answer 9b.)
   9b. If no, why not? _____

_____

10. Please indicate how important you perceive each of the following factors as it relates to your buying decision. Please rank-order the following factors from 1 to 5, where 1 is the most important and 5 is the least important.
   _____ Product quality   _____ Price   _____ Delivery
   _____ Breadth of products offered   _____ XYZ Foods branded products (Riceman)

11. What trade magazines do you read on a regular basis? (Please check all that apply.)
   ❏ World of Woks   ❏ Stir-Fry Today   ❏ Soy Sauce Times
   ❏ Restaurant News   ❏ Frozen Food Age   ❏ Julia Childs' Guide to Woks
   ❏ Other: _____

12. Are you aware of any XYZ Foods ads in these magazines?
   ❏ Yes   ❏ No

13. Please rate your level of satisfaction with XYZ Foods in the areas listed below. Circle the number that best corresponds to your assessment of that particular area. Additional comments are welcome to the right of the response. Should more space be required, please feel free to insert an additional page.

1 = Excellent   2 = Good   3 = Fair   4 = Poor   5 = Not applicable/don't know

Comments

Breadth of products offered. 1	2	3	4	5	_____
Branded products. 1	2	3	4	5	_____
Product quality 1	2	3	4	5	_____
Price 1	2	3	4	5	_____
Value. 1	2	3	4	5	_____
Salespeople 1	2	3	4	5	_____
Delivery. 1	2	3	4	5	_____
Contact with shipping department. . . . 1	2	3	4	5	_____
Contact with credit department 1	2	3	4	5	_____
Phone calls handled efficiently 1	2	3	4	5	_____
Phone calls handled courteously 1	2	3	4	5	_____

14. Do you have a current copy of the XYZ Foods price list/advertising flyer?
    ❑ Yes (Answer 14a.)   ❑ No   ❑ Don't know
     14a. If yes, do you find our price list/advertising flyer to be a useful document?
       ❑ Yes   ❑ No (Answer 14b.)
     14b. If no, what could we do to improve it? _____
     _____
     _____

15. Is it useful to you for XYZ Foods to have a booth at trade shows?
    ❑ Yes (Answer 15a.)   ❑ No (Answer 15a.)
     15a. Why or why not? _____
     _____

16. Please give your assessment of how XYZ Foods fares relative to its competition in the areas listed below. Circle the number that best corresponds to your assessment of that particular area. Additional comments are welcome to the right of and/or below the response. Should more space be required, please feel free to insert an additional page.

1 = Better   2 = The same   3 = Worse   4 = Not applicable/don't know

Comments

Breadth of products offered. 1	2	3	4	_____
Branded products. 1	2	3	4	_____
Product quality 1	2	3	4	_____
Price 1	2	3	4	_____
Value. 1	2	3	4	_____
Salespeople 1	2	3	4	_____

Delivery	1	2	3	4	_____
Contact with shipping department . . .	1	2	3	4	_____
Contact with credit department	1	2	3	4	_____
Phone calls handled efficiently.	1	2	3	4	_____
Phone calls handled courteously	1	2	3	4	_____

Additional Comments: _____

_____

_____

_____

17. What future trends in the stir-fry industry do you expect to have a positive influence on your business?

_____

_____

_____

   17a. How would you rate XYZ Foods' responsiveness to these positive trends?
   ❏ Excellent   ❏ Good   ❏ Fair   ❏ Poor   ❏ Don't know

   Please explain: _____

   _____

18. What future trends in the stir-fry industry do you expect to have a negative influence on your business?

_____

_____

_____

   18a. How would you rate XYZ Foods' responsiveness to these negative trends? _____
   ❏ Excellent   ❏ Good   ❏ Fair   ❏ Poor   ❏ Don't know

   Please explain: _____

   _____

19. What do you perceive to be XYZ Foods' greatest strengths?

_____

_____

_____

20. What do you perceive to be XYZ Foods' major weaknesses?

_____

_____

_____

21. What are your suggestions for improving XYZ Foods?

_____

_____

_____

Thank you for your help. It is greatly appreciated.

Please return this questionnaire to the address below. A business-reply envelope has been provided for your convenience. Remember your response is important to us and will be kept completely confidential.

XYZ FOODS, INC.
c/o Any Research Firm, Inc.
P.O. Box 12345
Anytown, U.S.A. 12345-6789

FIGURE 3.4   Sample Questionnaire #2

Company Description   The business that used the following questionnaire is a regionally based company that provides insurance-related products.

Objectives   The objectives of the customer assessment included the following:

- Obtain profile of customers.

- How do clients hear of the company (effectiveness of advertising/promotional efforts)?

- What is the purchasing profile—coverage purchased through the company organization versus other companies.

- Measure effectiveness of agents.

- Assess overall service provided.

- Identify perceived strengths and weaknesses.

- Solicit suggestions for improvement.

XM BROWN & COMPANY

INSURANCE

Dear Valued Client,

We sincerely appreciate your business and the opportunity to satisfy your insurance needs. In an effort to better serve our clients, we request your help in evaluating our performance.

We have engaged the independent marketing research firm of Any Research Firm, Inc., to conduct this survey. Please take a few minutes and fill out the attached questionnaire. Your responses will help us serve you better. As a valued client, your input is essential for our accurate evaluation. Your willingness to cooperate with this review of our company is greatly appreciated. *All responses will be kept completely confidential.*

For your convenience, enclosed is a postage-paid envelope for the return of the questionnaire. To allow for timely processing, please return the survey within seven days of receipt.

In advance, we would like to thank you for your assistance.

Sincerely,

Xavier M. Brown
President

1234 E. SOUTH STREET • DENVER, COLORADO 12345-6789 • (303)123-4567

Client Questionnaire

1. How long have you been a client?
   ❏ Less than 1 year   ❏ 1 to 2 years   ❏ 3 to 5 years   ❏ More than 5 years

2. Are you a personal client or business client?
   ❏ Personal   ❏ Business
   2a. If you are a business client
      ❏ Corporation   ❏ Partnership
      ❏ Sole proprietor   ❏ Other:_____

3. Annual Premium Range:
   ❏ Less than $500   ❏ $500 to $1000   ❏ $1,001 to $5,000   ❏ $5,001 to $10,000
   ❏ $10,001 to $50,000 ❏ $50,001 to   ❏ $100,001 to   ❏ Over $200,000
                          $100,000 $200,000

4. How did you find out about this insurance agency?
   ❏ Word of mouth   ❏ Referral   ❏ Newspaper   ❏ Radio advertisement
   ❏ Noticed our office ❏ Know one of our agents. If so, which one? _____
   ❏ Other: _____

5. Please list the two most important factors you looked for when selecting our agency.

    1. _____

    2. _____

6. How would you categorize the premiums you pay for your policy/policies?

    ❏ High   ❏ Reasonable   ❏ Low

    Please comment: _____

7. Please indicate your awareness and interest in the following types of coverage offered by XM Brown & Company.

    Please check the appropriate box on each line. A box that is not checked will be considered a "no" answer.

	I have purchased this policy from XM Brown & Company.	I have purchased this policy from another company.	I have not purchased this policy, but it is of interest to me.
Accident/health (group)	❏	❏	❏
Auto/motorcycle	❏	❏	❏
Aviation	❏	❏	❏
Boat/yacht	❏	❏	❏
Broiler/machinery	❏	❏	❏
Bond/builder's risk	❏	❏	❏
Professional/directors' and officers' liability	❏	❏	❏
Homeowners/Renters/ Mobile home owners	❏	❏	❏
Inland marine	❏	❏	❏
IRA/Keogh/TSA/ annuities	❏	❏	❏
Life insurance/ disability income	❏	❏	❏
Umbrella	❏	❏	❏
Workers' compensation	❏	❏	❏

8. What other types of insurance would you purchase from XM Brown & Company if available?

_____

_____

9. Have you ever considered changing insurance agencies?

    ❏ Yes   ❏ No

    If yes, why? _____

_____

10. Do you currently use any other agency for your insurance needs?

    If yes, why? _____

_____

11. Do you feel that our phones are answered in a professional manner? _____

    ❏ Yes   ❏ No

    Please comment: _____

12. Please rate the effectiveness of your XM Brown & Company *agent*. Circle the number that best corresponds to your assessment of that particular area. Additional comments are welcome to the right of the response. Should more space be required, please feel free to insert an additional page.

    1 = Excellent   2 = Good   3 = Fair   4 = Poor   5 = Not applicable/don't know

					Comments
Accessibility	1	2	3	4	5	_____
Competence	1	2	3	4	5	_____
Frequency of contact	1	2	3	4	5	_____
Keeps client informed	1	2	3	4	5	_____
Personality	1	2	3	4	5	_____
Handles problems effectively	1	2	3	4	5	_____
Policy knowledge	1	2	3	4	5	_____
Professionalism	1	2	3	4	5	_____
Promptness	1	2	3	4	5	_____
Reliability	1	2	3	4	5	_____
Returns phone calls	1	2	3	4	5	_____
Understands client needs	1	2	3	4	5	_____

13. Please rate the overall service you receive from XM Brown & Company, please rate your agent's ability tolain the policy to you.

    ❏ Excellent   ❏ Good   ❏ Fair   ❏ Poor

    Please comment: _____

14. Upon purchasing your policy/policies from XM Brown & Company, please rate your agent's ability to explain the policy to you.

    ❏ Excellent   ❏ Good   ❏ Fair   ❏ Poor

    Please comment: _____

15. Would you like your agent to call on you again to further explain your policy/policies?

    ❏ Yes   ❏ No

16. If you have ever experienced a loss and had to make a claim with XM Brown & Company, how would you rate the service provided?

    ❏ Excellent   ❏ Good   ❏ Fair   ❏ Poor   ❏ Not applicable/don't know

17. How would you rate the service provided by our customer service representatives?

    ❏ Excellent   ❏ Good   ❏ Fair   ❏ Poor   ❏ Not applicable/don't know

18. Which of the customer service representatives have you dealt with?

    _____

19. Are you comfortable dealing with our customer service representatives?

    ❑ Yes   ❑ No   ❑ Not applicable/don't know

    If not, why?_____

    _____

20. Our current office hours are 8:00 A.M. to 4:30 P.M. Monday through Friday. Do you perceive a need for us to establish additional office hours?

    ❑ Yes   ❑ No

    Please comment: _____

21. Would you recommend XM Brown & Company to others?

    ❑ Yes   ❑ No

22. Have you recommended XM Brown & Company to others?

    ❑ Yes   ❑ No

23. What do you consider to be this agency's greatest strengths?

    _____

    _____

24. What do you consider to be this agency's greatest weaknesses?

    _____

    _____

25. What are your suggestions for improving XM Brown & Company?

    _____

    _____

Thank you for your help. It is greatly appreciated.

If you are interested in receiving more information about any of our services listed in question 7, please provide your name and address below. This is not required to complete the questionnaire.

Area(s) of interest: _____

Name: _____

Address: _____

City, State, Zip: _____

Please return this questionnaire to us in the postage-paid envelope. Thank you.

FIGURE 3.5   Response Letter to Customers

Dear Customers:

I would like to sincerely thank all of you who took part in our recent assessment of customer satisfaction.

I would like to share with you some of the results:

- Result A
- Result B   (*Cite results that were particularly positive.*)
- Result C, etc.

While we are very proud of the high esteem in which you hold our firm, there are some areas that are not at the level we would like. Based on excellent feedback from you, we are in the process of making modifications. Some of these modifications are as follows:

- Modification A
- Modification B   (*Share specific modifications and the timetable for implementation.*)
- Modification C, etc.

Thank you for your input. We will continue to work hard to provide you with superior products and services. We sincerely appreciate your business.

Sincerely,

President

Notes on Using the Assessment

The assessment exercise is not intended to be all-inclusive; each organization and the market in which it operates is unique. The questions raised are intended to help an organization go beyond the facade of "rationalizing" its action or inaction. The assessment tools provided herein are intended to be insightful. It is important that each organization determine the specific relevance of the assessment with respect to its specific situation.

Scoring the Assessment

Filling Out the Form

1. If the statement is generally true of your organization, mark the "yes" column.
2. If the statement is not true of your organization, mark the "no" column.
3. If the statement is occasionally true of your organization, mark the "sometimes" column.
4. If a particular statement does not have relevance to your organization or if information is not available for a credible response, then draw a line through the statement.

Evaluating the Responses

1. A negative answer is seldom favorable. It indicates an absence of a particular activity that may or may not be compensated for elsewhere.
2. A positive answer is almost always favorable. However, too many "yes" answers may indicate that your response is not sufficiently objective.
3. Several "sometimes" answers may point to a lack of direction or commitment.
4. Several "crossed off" questions may indicate insufficient records or an inadequate data base.

Rating the Responses

1. Upon completion of the assessment form, award points as follows:
   - For each "yes" answer, award one point.
   - For each "sometimes" answer, award one-half point.
   - For each "no" answer, award zero points.
   - For each question crossed off the list, award zero points, and deduct one from the total number of questions in the assessment.
2. Divide the total number of points awarded by the number of questions on the assessment (less the number of questions crossed off the list).

$$\text{Score} = \frac{\text{Number of points awarded}}{\text{Number of questions answered}}$$

A score of 1 is excellent. Scores less than 1 should be evaluated with respect to their distance from 1. The farther the score is from 1, the more removed the organization is from initiating actions that are beneficial to superior customer service.

Setting Objectives Assessment

Organization: _____ Date: _____ Person Conducting Assessment: _____

	Yes	No	Sometimes
1. The purpose of the research project is determined prior to its derivation and implementation.	_____	_____	_____
2. When evaluating customer satisfaction, the organization sets realistic goals.	_____	_____	_____
3. The organization tries to objectively understand the customer's perspective.	_____	_____	_____
4. A clear purpose underlies each customer survey.	_____	_____	_____
5. The organization clearly formulates its assessment objectives prior to considering different methodologies.	_____	_____	_____
6. When forming objectives, the organization obtains employee input.	_____	_____	_____
7. The organization reviews selected objectives to confirm that useful data will be gathered.	_____	_____	_____
8. In selecting objectives, the organization seeks information that will enable it to improve customer satisfaction.	_____	_____	_____
9. Objectives are consistent with the goals and policies of the organization.	_____	_____	_____
10. The organization is committed to objectives that will truly reveal status and performance.	_____	_____	_____

Page total: _____ + _____ + _____ = ☐

Page 1 Total: =   ☐

Exercise Total: =   ☐

Choosing the Best Survey Technique

During a trade show, two small manufacturers find themselves sit-
ting next to each other in a seminar dealing with the importance of
providing excellent customer service. A key concept stressed repeat-
edly during the seminar is the importance of measuring customer sat-
isfaction.

Bob, a small parts manufacturer from California, shares with
John, a manufacturer from Minnesota, that he tried to implement a
way of measuring customer satisfaction a few years ago but found it
to be costly and unproductive. The method he used involved focus
groups. John, on the other hand says that his efforts at measuring cus-
tomer satisfaction have been very cost-effective and productive for his
firm. He has used periodic written surveys and an 800 number.

When asked how he decided on using those particular methods,
John says that the firm he commissioned to help conduct the measure-
ments carefully reviewed with him the objectives of the study and then
decided on the appropriate methodologies.

Approximately 18 months later, Bob and John's paths cross at a re-
gional show. Bob shares that he has implemented a comprehensive on-
going customer satisfaction measurement program that consists
primarily of periodic telephone surveys. The program has helped the
firm considerably.

There are many techniques available that will allow you and your company to obtain valuable customer information. Regardless of the objectives of your particular assessment, the techniques described in the pages that follow can be helpful to you. Remember that it is important to assess the various techniques in terms of how they meet your specific needs with respect to the type of information your organization is seeking, the characteristics of the respondents targeted and the best survey method to use. (See Figure 4.1.) When deciding on a survey method, remember to consider cost, resources, your time frame, capabilities, etc.

There are many techniques available to companies of all sizes. The following discussion explains some of the more straightforward techniques.

Telephone Surveys

Phone surveys are excellent methods to use if time is of the essence, the questions are not intrusive and the survey is not too long.

Great care must be taken to ensure accuracy. For example, efforts must be made to verify the phone numbers with respect to the demographic profile being targeted. In addition, training must be thorough so that each phone surveyor asks questions in a consistent manner and records responses appropriately.

Although phone surveys are excellent "listening" tools, they have the following limitations:

- Some time may have passed since respondents were involved with the activity they are being questioned about, and consequently, they may have trouble quickly recalling some of the most pertinent details.

- Some telephone surveys have a tendency to be fast-paced, whether intended or not. Respondents and interviewers sometimes push the conversation forward in an attempt to eliminate dead time. This quick pace can result in short, truncated answers to open-ended questions.

- Respondents may also have difficulty responding to questions over the telephone that involve a response scale. With no visual aid, they may have difficulty keeping track of the possible responses.

- Extensive effort is involved in constructing a well-designed telephone survey. However, the validity of the survey can be negatively

FIGURE 4.1 Diagram of the Important Interrelationships in the Design and Selection of a Measurement Instrument

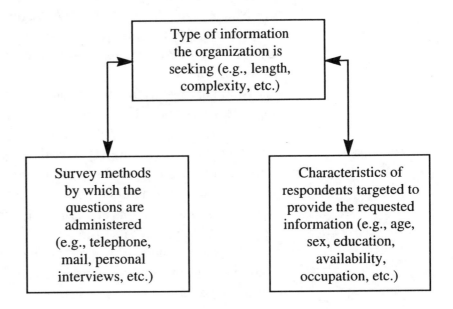

affected if the interviewers do not follow directions properly. For example, sometimes interviewers read questions incorrectly or lead respondents toward particular responses.

■ In most cases, respondents are not "waiting" for the survey call. In other words, they may be in a hurry to do something else and may feel the call is an intrusion. Such an attitude obviously will affect their responses.

A sample telephone survey is shown in Figure 4.2 at the end of the chapter.

Telephone Survey Tips

■ If long-distance calls are part of the survey, be aware of the various time zones.

■ The phone survey script should be carefully reviewed with all interviewers.

Mail Surveys

Mail surveys can be slightly longer than telephone surveys since respondents fill out the questionnaires at their leisure. When properly designed, written questionnaires eliminate the potential bias of interviewer error.

Mail surveys often allow businesses to receive a greater quantity of high-quality information. Since respondents complete these surveys at their leisure, they can check records, confirm with family or colleagues and take time to accurately recollect details. Respondents have the opportunity to think carefully about their responses and provide more information on open-ended questions. Mail surveys also allow respondents to answer questions anonymously while providing the business the opportunity to present itself in a high-quality, standardized manner.

There are, however, several limitations to mail surveys. First, the response rate on mail surveys is generally lower than other forms of research. Second, the questionnaire may get lost with other mail. Third, the respondent may not have time to complete the survey; or his or her intentions may be good, but the survey remains uncompleted. For a mail survey, it is also essential that the source information for the mailing list be accurate. Inaccurate mailing lists increase the cost per respondent and raise the risk of having an insufficient sample size, thereby rendering the information received useless.

Mail Survey Tips

- Quality and attractiveness of piece
- Persuasiveness of the message
- Curiosity and spirit of cooperation created
- Good graphics
- A brief, well-written cover letter

Face-to-Face Personal Interviews

One of the simplest ways to assess customer satisfaction is by interviewing customers and asking what they like and don't like about your company, products or services as well as what they perceive to be your strengths and weaknesses.

An advantage of the personal interview is that respondents can examine, touch or handle a product. The interviewer can then observe first-hand their reactions and ask follow-up questions. Personal interviewing is the primary information-gathering method for projects that require direct contact, special knowledge, a specific location or a unique set of limiting characteristics for respondents who qualify for the survey.

While personal interviews are very effective, a primary drawback is that they generally require a field force of interviewers in order to complete enough interviews within a given period of time. This force of interviewers usually is recruited from within a company or is obtained from an outside firm. Personal interviews are also very expensive (per respondent), particularly if the sample is spread over a wide geographic area.

Finally, considerable care must be taken in training interviewers in the correct interviewing and recording procedures. Interviewers must also have a thorough knowledge of the specific characteristics and requirements of the project. Plans should be made to provide sufficient levels of field supervision, and field interviewers must take considerable care to avoid introducing various biases.

Personal Interview Tips

- The interviewer must have a professional appearance.
- The participant should be given a brief explanation of the study and the role he or she is expected to play.
- Participants should feel that both the study and their responses are important.

A chart comparing personal interviews, telephone surveys and mail surveys is provided in Figure 4.3 at the end of the chapter.

Focus Groups

Focus groups consist of individuals brought together to participate in discussions concerning a series of topics, questions or products. The individuals usually are selected by demographic characteristics. A moderator directs the questions and line of discussion and asks probing follow-up questions. Focus groups are particularly effective when dealing with new-product introductions, particular product features and benefits, as well as other issues.

Although focus groups are effective in some situations, they do have limitations. For example, many meetings are often required to produce a sufficiently valid sample. Factors that can affect validity include the following:

- A dominant person who sways the opinions of others within the group
- An ineffective moderator
- The limitations of the participants (e.g., improper screening or insufficient dialogue)

Compensating for such limitations usually requires numerous cycles of focus groups, thereby raising costs appreciably.

Focus groups also make it difficult to reach a much larger cross-section of the client base. And at times it is difficult to protect the identity of the respondents. In some settings respondents may not feel they have sufficient time to reflect on questions before responding due to feeling pressured to answer the questions quickly.

Focus Group Tips

- Carefully select 10 to 12 participants with common backgrounds or experience with the subject of the interview.
- Choose a moderator who is sensitive to group members' feelings but also proficient in leading the group through a productive discussion.
- Explain the subject matter to be discussed at the beginning of the session.
- Introduce participants to one another.
- Provide name tags for participants.
- Sessions should be less than 90 minutes in length.
- Arrange for a tape and/or video recording of the session.

Mystery Shopping

Mystery shopping uses people unknown to company personnel to visit the facility, call in by phone, talk to employees or talk to other customers to assess first impressions, service and product knowledge. Mystery shopping programs can help your company learn about customers' needs, evaluate current programs monitor new programs and evaluate training effectiveness.

However, in order to be effective, mystery shopping programs must have a significant pool of "shoppers" collecting sufficient data over a period of time. In addition, if a shopper is recognized, that shopper cannot return to the facility again since his or her identity has been compromised. It is imperative that shoppers be well trained so that they have a standard series of evaluation items that are being looked at and a standard rating scale so that recipients of the information can use it for comparative purposes. Great care must be taken so that shoppers do not introduce personal bias into their evaluations (unless requested in specific instances).

Toll-Free Numbers

Toll-free numbers (800 numbers) are a great way to solve problems early. They enable customers with problems to immediately "let off steam" rather than having it build unspoken and unresolved. Toll-free numbers are also a great tool for gathering marketing intelligence from customers concerning what they think about new ideas, trends, suggestions, etc. Thus, it is important that a company make its 800 number widely available to customers.

Toll-free numbers are excellent tools for measuring customer satisfaction. But to be truly effective, you must have a knowledgeable person answering the phone who can resolve a complaint, answer a question, take an order or provide accurate information. Otherwise, your best intentions are wasted. In fact, your business may actually exacerbate levels of frustration if a dissatisfied customer calls your number with a problem and an uninformed person answers the phone.

Comment and Complaint Cards

Comment and complaint cards can be very useful if they are well designed and are used along with an overall customer satisfaction assessment strategy. Gathering the cards without a comprehensive assessment program imposes an unnecessary burden upon the respondent.

But when used along with a comprehensive assessment program, these cards are an excellent way to survey your customers. For example, when combined with surveys, the comments can provide a continuing index of customer experiences and attitudes over time.

Frontline Contact

Frontline contact refers to any opportunities where rank and file employees are provided an opportunity to spend time with customers in an informal setting (a reception, coffee and donuts, dinner, etc.). Although usually not relevant from a quantitative standpoint, frontline contact provides an excellent forum for gathering ideas for improvement. Such interaction also removes much of the mystery from the relationship between the business and its customers since communication is enhanced by personal contact.

Mutual Education

A training opportunity of any kind (e.g., customers coming to your facility for training or your employees going out into the field to train or be trained) provides a good opportunity for measuring customer satisfaction. Such classes are an excellent way to listen and learn from your customers, regardless of who is doing the training. During such training, your employees can regularly inquire about what they can do to be of better service.

FIGURE 4.2   Sample Telephone Survey

Fast-Food Customer Satisfaction Survey

Name of interviewer: _____

Questionnaire #: _____

Phone Number called: _____

Date/time: _____

Hello, my name is _____. I am conducting a survey regarding customer satisfaction with restaurants in our area. It will only take a few minutes of your time. Your answers will remain anonymous. Would you mind if I asked you a few questions?

[Wait for response.]

	Circle:
If "yes," politely end call.	1
If "no," continue.	

Many people use the words *fast food* to describe certain restaurants.

1. In the context of restaurants, what do the words *fast food* mean to you? [Probe.]

   _____

   _____

   _____

2. In a typical month, approximately how often do you visit a fast-food restaurant? [Do not read options.]

	Circle:
Never (Skip to question 7.)	1
Less than once a month (Skip to question 7.)	2
1 to 2 times (Continue.)	3
3 to 4 times (Continue.)	4
5 to 9 times (Continue.)	5
10 times or more (Continue.)	6

3. Which fast-food restaurant do you go to most frequently? Why? [Probe.]

   _____

   _____

   _____

4. Do you remember seeing or hearing any advertisements for fast-food restaurants in the last few weeks?

	Circle:
No (Skip to question 6.)	1
Yes (Continue.)	2

5. Do you remember which restaurants you recall seeing or hearing the advertisements for? Any others?

   ❑ Check if didn't see.

   First mention: _____

   Second mention: _____

   Third mention: _____

6. I would like to ask you to rate fast-food restaurants that specialize in _____ with respect to customer service. Considering the type of fast-food restaurants that you have recently visited, would you say that the [insert first item below] at these restaurants is [are] excellent, good, fair, poor? [Then repeat for each listed attribute.]

		Excellent	*Good*	*Fair*	*Poor*
a.	Quality of service provided	1	2	3	4
b.	Speed of service	1	2	3	4
c.	Courtesy of employees	1	2	3	4
d.	Cleanliness of the restaurant	1	2	3	4
e.	Value for price paid	1	2	3	4
f.	Quality of food	1	2	3	4
g.	Prices of food	1	2	3	4

7. In closing, I would like to ask you a few questions that will help classify the answers given. As stated before, all of your responses are being treated anonymously.

   Are there any children under the age of 15 living in your home?

	Circle:
No (Skip to question 9.)	1
Yes (Continue.)	2

8. In what age category do you fall? [Read categories.]

	Circle:
18 and under	1
19 to 24	2
25 to 34	3
35 to 49	4
50 to 65	5
Over 65	6
Refused	7

9. Is the total household income under or over $25,000?

	Circle:
Over	1
Under	2

Thank you very much for your time and input.

Interviewer: Record sex.

10.

	Circle:
Male	1
Female	2

FIGURE 4.3   Comparison Chart

The relative strengths and weaknesses of the three primary methods of conducting survey-based customer satisfaction research are highlighted below.

Characteristic	Personal Interview	Telephone Survey	Mail Survey
Response rate	+	+	-
Overall cost	-	+	+
Ability to acquire complex information	+	o	-
Ability to use visual aids	+	-	o
Ability to probe for more detailed response	+	o	-
Ability to control situation in which response is made	+	o	-
Ability to acquire lengthy information	+	-	o
Ability to control phrasing of questions	o	o	+
Ability to offer anonymity to respondent	-	-	+
Ability to provide immediate incentive	+	-	+
Avoidance of errors caused by respondent-interviewer interaction	-	-	+
Time required for completion of survey	-	+/-	+/-
Ability to reach a population that is geographically dispersed	-	+	+

Key:
> (+) = comparative strength.
> (-) = comparative weakness.
> (o) = no comparative strength or weakness/not applicable.

Notes on Using the Assessment

The assessment exercise is not intended to be all-inclusive; each organization and the market in which it operates is unique. The questions raised are intended to help an organization go beyond the facade of "rationalizing" its action or inaction. The assessment tools provided herein are intended to be insightful. It is important that each organization determine the specific relevance of the assessment with respect to its specific situation.

Scoring the Assessment

Filling Out the Form

1. If the statement is generally true of your organization, mark the "yes" column.
2. If the statement is not true of your organization, mark the "no" column.
3. If the statement is occasionally true of your organization, mark the "sometimes" column.
4. If a particular statement does not have relevance to your organization or if information is not available for a credible response, then draw a line through the statement.

Evaluating the Responses

1. A negative answer is seldom favorable. It indicates an absence of a particular activity that may or may not be compensated for elsewhere.
2. A positive answer is almost always favorable. However, too many "yes" answers may indicate that your response is not sufficiently objective.
3. Several "sometimes" answers may point to a lack of direction or commitment.
4. Several "crossed off" questions may indicate insufficient records or an inadequate data base.

Rating the Responses

1. Upon completion of the assessment form, award points as follows:
   - For each "yes" answer, award one point.
   - For each "sometimes" answer, award one-half point.
   - For each "no" answer, award zero points.
   - For each question crossed off the list, award zero points, and deduct one from the total number of questions in the assessment.
2. Divide the total number of points awarded by the number of questions on the assessment (less the number of questions crossed off the list).

$$\text{Score} = \frac{\text{Number of points awarded}}{\text{Number of questions answered}}$$

A score of 1 is excellent. Scores less than 1 should be evaluated with respect to their distance from 1. The farther the score is from 1, the more removed the organization is from initiating actions that are beneficial to superior customer service.

Assessment of Methodologies

Organization: _____   Date: _____   Person Conducting Assessment: _____

	Yes	No	Sometimes
1. When initiating a research project to evaluate customer satisfaction, the organization carefully reviews the methodologies available and selects the one that best matches the objectives of the project.	_____	_____	_____
2 Prior to final selection of a methodology, the organization confirms that the methodology is consistent with its image.	_____	_____	_____
3. The organization exercises great caution in assuming that no bias is introduced into the process.	_____	_____	_____
4. If an outside firm is retained to conduct the analysis, the organization is careful to confirm that it is competent in the selected methodology.	_____	_____	_____
5. Employees are given the opportunity to offer input concerning the selection of methodology.	_____	_____	_____
6. When selecting a methodology, the organization takes comparative capabilities (with previous or subsequent studies) into account.	_____	_____	_____
7. When selecting a methodology, the organization gives careful consideration to whether it wants inferential or descriptive data.	_____	_____	_____
8. When selecting a methodology, the organization is sensitive to the time impact on existing, potential and past customers.	_____	_____	_____

Page total: _____ + _____ + _____ = ☐

9. Prior to making a final methodology selection, the organization carefully reviews financial requirements.

    —————   —————   —————

10. Management is actively involved in the selection of methodology.

    —————   —————   —————

    Page total: ————— + ————— + ————— = ⬜

    Page 1 Total: =   ⬜

    Page 2 Total: =   ⬜
    _____

    Exercise Total: =   ⬜

What You Need To Know about Statistics

Judy is a successful retailer in a large southern city. As a hard-working entrepreneur and one desirous of being innovative in her field, she sets out to implement a program to measure customer satisfaction.

To save money, Judy produces and implements the measurement instrument herself. To her credit, the instrument has excellent graphics and is very attractive. She obtains an excellent response rate.

However, in spite of her best efforts, she finds out that the data she has collected is not usable. Unbeknownst to Judy, she has made several errors that have invalidated the data:

- *She and her staff went through the customer list and personally picked those to whom they wanted the questionnaires sent.*
- *Several questions had more than one item per question.*
- *Several questions were asked in a biased manner.*

The end result is that Judy actually cost herself time and money by not adhering to good statistical principles.

The previous chapter explained several techniques that can be used to gather information about customer satisfaction. Although these techniques can be very useful, they can also be misused and can cause problems.

This chapter is designed to help you and your business become informed about statistical claims and findings. When properly derived and used, they can be a powerful tool for your business. But when improperly derived, statistical information can lead to distorted findings and inappropriate applications.

Validity

A survey is valid if it measures what (and only what) it is intended to measure. It must not be influenced by irrelevant factors that bias (push or pull) the results in one particular direction. By introducing a bias and variables other than those being measured, the results can be influenced and invalidated.

Bias

One of the most prevalent and detrimental aspects of any survey is bias. Questions are considered biased if they are worded in a way that pulls the respondent in one direction over another. Bias can occur in many different ways and is so powerful that it can invalidate a question or even an entire study.

To avoid bias, you must carefully screen and check all questions. Each question should measure only a single variable. In most cases (unless otherwise stated), questions are designed so the respondent can present a specific reply, rather than a general one.

Causes of Bias

Leading Questions   Leading questions are a source of bias because they tend to lead the respondent in a particular direction. For example: "Don't you agree that this is a top-quality law firm?"

Loaded Questions   Loaded questions differ from leading questions in that they are more subtle and tend to offer a reason for responding in a particular way. For example: "Do you advocate higher fees so we can stay in business?"

In this case, the respondents are placed in a difficult position. If they respond positively to the question, they are advocating higher fees whether they want them or not. On the other hand, a negative response suggests that they may be willing to let the firm go out of business.

Detail Respondents shouldn't be asked to recall too much detail. If it has been a long time since a respondent has been involved in a particular activity, the exact measurement of a behavior may not be possible. For example: "In the last five years, exactly how many times have you contacted our office by phone?"

While this may be an important piece of information, asking the customer to respond with an exact number may be an unrealistic expectation.

Ambiguity Different words can mean different things to different people. The following example points out the importance of selecting words that mean the same thing to everyone: "Do you ever eat dinner on the clubhouse terrace?"

While this sounds like an innocent question, the word "dinner" may be ambiguous. Some respondents may interpret "dinner" to mean an evening meal, while others may think of it as an afternoon meal. And the menus may be different at the different time slots! In this example, a simple misinterpretation of "dinner" can invalidate the question.

Response Scale Bias can be introduced if a question offers a response scale that is slanted toward a certain answer. For example:

How would you rate the fairness of fees charged?

❑ Excellent   ❑ Good   ❑ Fair   ❑ Poor

By not placing "excellent" on the same line as the other choices, the respondent is apt to select that response over "good," "fair" or "poor," thereby creating bias.

Response Bias

Response bias, which is one of the most common forms of bias, is caused by the respondent's attitude and predisposition. It is possible to control some forms of response bias by carefully selecting appropriate vocabulary and by placing the questions in a particular sequence. Response bias can take any of the following forms:

- "Correct" response is perceived as being socially acceptable.
- Questions are slanted to avoid controversy.
- Questions are threatening.
- Questions have a particular sequence.

Nonresponse Bias

One of the most serious concerns for anyone conducting a research study is the problem of low response. Many researchers express concern about people who do not respond. How do the answers of those who respond differ from those who do not respond, and what inferences can you draw from that information?

Nonresponse bias is not an issue if those who failed to respond to the survey represent a random portion of the sample. In most studies, however, this is not the case. An individual's demographic profile and the strength of his or her attitudes and perceptions may influence response. Respondents may overrepresent some groups and underrepresent others. The following example of two sets of results will help illustrate this point:

Athletic Club ABC is interested in expanding its membership and has decided to begin a promotional campaign. Management decides to advertise by direct mail and purchases a mailing list of 1,000 names from a local vendor. The board of directors decides that the best approach is to compile a brief questionnaire and mail it to everyone on the list. The board indicates that it is primarily interested in finding out the level of interest in the club from individuals throughout the community.

First analysis: One thousand questionnaires are mailed and 100 are returned, representing a 10 percent response rate. Of the 100, 50 respondents indicate an interest in the athletic club, and 50 do not. This level of return might lead the board of directors to conclude that 50 percent of the sample group is interested in their club. But that 50 percent may or may not exceed the actual number of local residents interested in joining an athletic club.

Second analysis: Of the 1,000 questionnaires, 500 are returned, representing a 50 percent response rate. Results indicate that 50 respondents (or 10 percent) are interested in joining an athletic club, and 90 percent are not. While highly unlikely, the possibility exists that everyone interested in joining an athletic club responded to the survey. Had all 1,000 surveys been returned, the 50 respondents would then represent only 5 percent of the sample.

This example shows that people who do not respond introduce nonresponse bias. You must acknowledge these individuals in any summary of information. Steps should be taken to minimize nonresponse bias by designing research instruments that positively represent organizations and encourage respondent participation. It is also important to insist on a random sample and to obtain a breakdown of the subgroups represented in the measurement sample.

Fatigue

If a survey is too lengthy, respondents may get tired and lose interest. Therefore, consider the possibility of respondent fatigue, and make any modifications necessary prior to releasing a measurement instrument to a target group.

Sampling

In some circumstances it may be possible for your firm to survey all your customers. But in many instances, budgetary constraints or a large customer base may make it difficult to perform an analysis of the whole population. The alternative is to survey only part—or a *sample*—of the customer base.

Your organization may elect to narrow the focus of your study by choosing to analyze a specific subgroup of the population. This type of analysis can be effective, and it can enable you to make inferences about a small portion of the population.

Random sampling is the most common method used for creating a diverse sample from the entire population. A *random sample* is one that selects a portion of all customers in a completely random fashion so that every customer has an equal chance of being selected. Your company may have 10,000 customers, but your budget for a particular analysis may only allow you to sample only 500. You can produce significant results if the 500 respondents are selected in random order.

Methods of randomly selecting a sample can be as simple as pulling names out of a hat or as sophisticated as programming a computer to select respondents. It is not advantageous for you to handpick the sample. If the sample consists of only the best customers or includes only your closest friends, business associates and members of your family, it will be biased. The analysis will then lose its validity, and the results will be meaningless.

Population Size versus Sample Size

One of the more complicated mathematical principles associated with research is the relationship between population size and sample size. The complication occurs because of the analytical importance of sample size versus the general irrelevance of population size.

As a general rule, it is safe to conclude that the larger the sample, the more precise are the estimates about the population. The larger sample more accurately reflects the population because it contains subjects from all possible subgroups. However, this does not mean that the sample must be a large percentage of the population. The laws of mathematical probability and statistics apply adequately to small and large samples and make population size relatively unimportant. This is a difficult concept for many to understand. The following example will help illustrate this point:

> Suppose there is a bag of colored marbles, into which you reach and pull out one blue marble. You would be foolish to conclude that all the marbles in the bag are blue. If you took a handful of ten marbles, of which four were blue and six were red, you would be somewhat safer in guessing that the bag contained more red than blue marbles. But if you cupped both hands together and brought out a total of 75 red and 25 blue marbles, you could be far more certain that the bag contained about three red marbles for each blue one.

In this example, mathematical principles suggest it doesn't matter if the bag of marbles was large or small. What matters is the size of the handful drawn as the sample (always assuming that the bag is well mixed and that any handful therefore was a true random sample).

Factors Influencing Sample Size

As has been previously mentioned, sample size is more important to the analytical process than population size. In addition, sample size can fluctuate depending on the demographics of the sample.

If the sample is a homogeneous group, in which the members of the group possess similar characteristics, the size of the sample required to perform a statistical analysis will decrease. For example, if the city council of City A wants to conduct a survey of its citizens and everyone living in that city is identical in every way, it will only be necessary to survey one person. That person will accurately reflect the views of every other citizen and provide the council with solid statistical data.

Conversely, if the sample is a heterogeneous group, in which members of the group are different from each other, a much larger sample is required. Depending on what the city council of City A wants to study, differences in age, gender, occupation, income and other variables need to be taken into account. Knowledge of these different characteristics is essential to obtaining a good cross section of the population.

Other factors that influence sample size are the cost considerations associated with a project. Your firm may elect to reduce the size of the sample on a particular analysis because of the costs of printing materials and postage. (The larger the sample, the more expensive the survey becomes.) You will spend less on postage and printing if you survey only 500 customers as opposed to 1,000.

The number of response categories associated with different types of questions can also influence sample size. A larger sample is required if there are more categories or responses available to respondents. A continuous response scale that offers many alternatives from which to choose enables respondents to distribute their answers over a wide range. An example is as follows:

1	2	3	4	5	6	7	8	9	10
Extremely Important								Not Important	

This type of response scale requires a large number of responses. On the other hand, questions that offer discrete response categories, such as yes/no questions, require a much smaller sample. Reducing the sample size provides a narrow range of responses, which brings the data closer together.

Variables

To create clear and concise questions, all measurement instruments should be carefully screened to avoid questions that contain more than one variable. A *variable* is the characteristic of a question that can take on more than one value—that is, it is subject to change. Each question should be written or asked with a specific purpose in mind. Never construct a question that leaves the respondent wondering what to do. For example:

Have you considered changing CPA and law firms?

❑ Yes   ❑ No

The respondent may be understandably confused by this question. He or she may think, "I have considered changing law firms but have never thought of changing CPA firms." How should the question be answered? It contains two different variables. In this case, the answer is partially "yes" and partially "no." But if the question is presented as two separate questions, the confusion is eliminated, and the respondent knows exactly how to answer.

Have you considered changing CPA firms?

❑ Yes   ❑ No

Have you considered changing law firms?

❑ Yes   ❑ No

Because of the difficulties they create, multivariable questions are invalid.

Relationships Between Variables

In statistical analysis, researchers attempt to describe individual variables. They not only want to know the nature of the individual variable but also the relationship between pairs of variables. For example, when a researcher wants to determine whether or not men and women differ in their opinions on a particular issue, he or she must assess the relationship between two variables: (1) the sex of the respondent and (2) their opinions on the issue.

When the responses to a pair of variables are compared to one another, two results are possible: (1) the answers move together, indicating they are related to one another; or (2) they move apart, indicating that there is no relationship between them. For a researcher to measure the relationship between variables, he or she must first determine the type of variable used as well as which variable is "dependent" and which is "independent."

To better understand the analyses that follow, here are some definitions of common variables:

- *Dependent variable.* The variable is potentially influenced, affected or determined by some other variable in a cause-and-effect relationship.

- *Independent variable.* The variable is the instrument that influences the values of another variable when there is a potential cause-and-effect relationship.

- *Continuous variable.* This variable represents a continuum (without any breaks or interruptions), so that the numeric values take on an infinite number of variables expressed in whole numbers and fractions.

- *Discrete variables.* A categorical variable that yields nominal data in no ordered relationship with other variables.

Statistical Analysis

When the data from different measurement methodologies has been collected, the process of analyzing it begins. It is important that generally accepted statistical procedures are used and that all phases of the analysis be easily understood. The analysis will not be useful to your business if its complexity of presentation is such that most people can't understand it.

For example, here are some questions from a survey produced by XYZ law firm:

1. What is your legal status (corporation, individual, partnership)?
2. What is your annual fee range?
3. How would you rate the overall quality of work received?

Using these questions as a reference point, a brief overview of some of the more common forms of quantitative analysis follows.

Frequencies

Frequencies indicate the number of respondents who selected each response, the percentage of each category of responses and how they relate to the entire group. Using the previous questions, frequencies would provide information regarding how many of the respondents were corporations (versus individuals or partnerships) or an indication of the various fee ranges.

Cross-Tabulations

Cross-tabulations evaluate the relationship between categorical variables. This type of analysis allows for a more homogeneous breakdown of the data—which can be more easily understood and interpreted.

For example, XYZ law firm wants to determine what segment of their client base responded "fair" to the question, "How would you rate the overall quality of work received?" Using all three previous questions, cross-tabulations will readily provide information about how corporations, individuals and partnerships responded to the quality of work received. In addition, quality of work can be assessed by determining how much corporations, individuals or partnerships spend annually on XYZ law firm.

This type of analysis will allow XYZ law firm to uncover and isolate possible problem areas within the firm. Corrective action can then be taken within departments that service particular clients.

Complex Statistical Analysis

Frequencies and cross-tabulations will not always provide you with a sufficient level of detail. You may need to utilize more complex types of analysis, such as correlation analysis, regression, confidence intervals and time-series analysis. These analyses require a greater knowledge of statistics and are best performed by an outside research firm. A brief summary of the types of complex statistical analysis is as follows:

Correlation Analysis Correlation analysis attempts to determine if a relationship exists between two continuous variables. If correlation analysis is of interest to you and your firm, you must know the size and direction of the correlation and whether or not it is statistically significant.

Regression Analysis Regression analysis is the technique used to measure the mathematical relationship between variables when one continuous variable is identified as an independent variable and another as a dependent variable.

Time-Series Analysis This is a set of measurements, ordered through time, on a particular quantity of interest. Specifically, time-series analysis measures how a particular variable fluctuates over time.

Confidence Intervals Confidence intervals are associated with a specified probability. The most commonly used measure is a 95 percent confidence interval. This means that there is a 95 percent probability that the figures for the entire population are within the stated range of the sample result. For example, the statement "The 95 percent confidence interval is 20 percent plus or minus 3 percent" means there is a 95 percent chance that the result for the entire population is between 17 percent and 23 percent.

General Guidelines for Your Research Efforts

Translate the Information Objectives

You and your colleagues may have mutually defined and clearly understood objectives. However, care must be exercised to ensure that such objectives are clearly represented in the questions asked.

Measurability

Observations made and questions asked must be specific and in a form that will facilitate comparison and analytical analysis now and in the future.

Subjectivity

Care should be taken in designing subjective questions so that while inquiring about people's thoughts on a particular subject, there are parameters established for the response.

Respondents Vary

Whenever information is sought through questioning, it is important to remember that respondents may vary widely with respect to education level, prejudices and moral persuasion, geographic differences and occupation. Thus, the measurement instrument must not only be designed with a particular focus in mind, but should also be carefully constructed so that it produces the type of information desired from the respondents.

Avoidance of Bias

Great care should be taken to avoid leading the respondent to a particular response. Bias can be introduced in the phrasing of a question or by the sequencing or positioning of possible responses.

Quantity of Information

Measurement instruments should be reviewed prior to their implementation. Be sure that sufficient information is sought from the respondents to allow for a thorough analysis consistent with the stated research objective. Also make sure the measurement instrument is not too long or complex because respondents may become fatigued, and this will have an impact on the quality of responses given.

FIGURE 5.1   Response Error Diagram

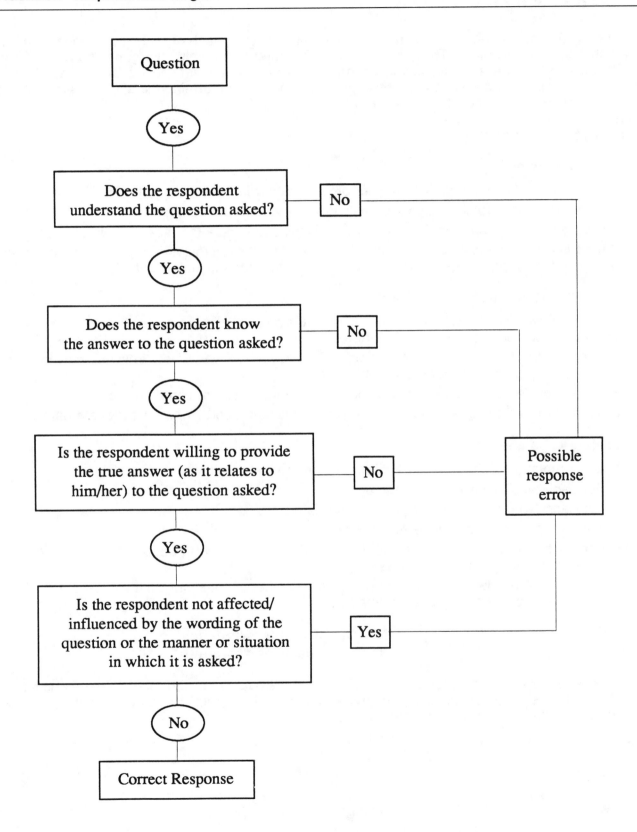

Notes on Using the Assessment

The assessment exercise is not intended to be all-inclusive; each organization and the market in which it operates is unique. The questions raised are intended to help an organization go beyond the facade of "rationalizing" its action or inaction. The assessment tools provided herein are intended to be insightful. It is important that each organization determine the specific relevance of the assessment with respect to its specific situation.

Scoring the Assessment

Filling Out the Form

1. If the statement is generally true of your organization, mark the "yes" column.
2. If the statement is not true of your organization, mark the "no" column.
3. If the statement is occasionally true of your organization, mark the "sometimes" column.
4. If a particular statement does not have relevance to your organization or if information is not available for a credible response, then draw a line through the statement.

Evaluating the Responses

1. A negative answer is seldom favorable. It indicates an absence of a particular activity that may or may not be compensated for elsewhere.
2. A positive answer is almost always favorable. However, too many "yes" answers may indicate that your response is not sufficiently objective.
3. Several "sometimes" answers may point to a lack of direction or commitment.
4. Several "crossed off" questions may indicate insufficient records or an inadequate data base.

Rating the Responses

1. Upon completion of the assessment form, award points as follows:
   - For each "yes" answer, award one point.
   - For each "sometimes" answer, award one-half point.
   - For each "no" answer, award zero points.
   - For each question crossed off the list, award zero points, and deduct one from the total number of questions in the assessment.
2. Divide the total number of points awarded by the number of questions on the assessment (less the number of questions crossed off the list).

$$\text{Score} = \frac{\text{Number of points awarded}}{\text{Number of questions answered}}$$

A score of 1 is excellent. Scores less than 1 should be evaluated with respect to their distance from 1. The farther the score is from 1, the more removed the organization is from initiating actions that are beneficial to superior customer service.

Statistics Assessment

Organization: _____ Date: _____ Person Conducting Assessment: _____

	Yes	No	Sometimes
1. The organization has conducted statistically valid studies of customer satisfaction.	_____	_____	_____
2. Bias has not been introduced into the analysis process.	_____	_____	_____
3. Measurement instruments are designed with the respondent in mind (e.g., length of instrument, complexity, objectives, etc.).	_____	_____	_____
4. After the study is completed, the targeted sample is informed of the results and what, if any, subsequent actions will be taken.	_____	_____	_____
5. Methods of distribution and collection of measurement instruments are carefully reviewed to preserve randomness.	_____	_____	_____
6. There is not more than one variable per question.	_____	_____	_____
7. The questions do not lead the respondent to any particular response.	_____	_____	_____
8. Results of customer satisfaction studies are carefully reviewed by management.	_____	_____	_____
9. Action plans are formulated from the input received from customers.	_____	_____	_____
10. Relevant data from the study are shared with employees.	_____	_____	_____

Page total: _____ + _____ + _____ = ☐

	Yes	No	Sometimes
11. The organization has a comprehensive plan for the measurement, management and enhancement of customer satisfaction.	————	————	————
12. Customer satisfaction is reviewed on a regular basis.	————	————	————
13. The organization has statistical benchmarks by which performance can be tracked over time.	————	————	————
14. Prior to implementing a study to measure customer satisfaction, the organization carefully reviews the best way to choose a sample.	————	————	————
15. The statistical output is presented in a readily understandable manner.	————	————	————

Page total: ———— + ———— + ———— = ☐

Page 1 Total: = ☐

Page 2 Total: = ☐

Exercise Total: = ☐

6

Distribution, Collection and Analysis of Surveys

Fred is the sales manager for a distributing firm located in the Northwest. He decides to launch a program to measure customer satisfaction. Excited about how the information may help the firm's selling efforts, Fred and his staff pursue the effort with enthusiasm but with a mandate from management to keep costs at a minimum.

To that end, the questionnaire is printed in a two-color format and is sent out bulk-rate, with no business-reply envelope. The effort produces a 6 percent response rate.

A year later Fred has the same questionnaire produced in a four-color format and sends it out via first-class mail. A business-reply envelope is enclosed. This effort produces a 48 percent response rate.

Critically important customer satisfaction information is of no benefit to your business unless it is effectively and efficiently distributed, collected, analyzed and disseminated to stakeholders (e.g., customers, employees, management, etc.).

Survey Distribution

Most people at one time or another have received a customer survey, and many have been unimpressed with the experience. Your research effort is but another contact with customers or potential customers. Each step in the research endeavor (distribution, collection, analysis and dissemination of results) must be well designed and implemented.

Mail Surveys

There are some important considerations to keep in mind about mail surveys.

Mail the Survey First-Class Many items that aren't mailed first-class remain unopened. Furthermore, consider what kind of message is conveyed to the recipient when items aren't mailed first-class: "Although we want you to take the time and effort to offer input, we did not care enough to send this survey first-class."

Send Notification That the Survey Is Coming In an era when virtually everyone suffers from lack of time, it is helpful to give advance notice. (An example of an advance notice letter is provided in Figure 6.1.)

Remind Recipients To Return Their Questionnaires If the questionnaire is not filled out soon after receipt, it may be misplaced or forgotten. Therefore, it is helpful to send a reminder postcard seven days after the questionnaire is sent. Tastefully done, such a reminder will prove effective in encouraging participation. (A sample reminder postcard is provided in Figure 6.2.)

Telephone Surveys

Sending advance notice of telephone surveys to targeted respondents may help position a research study by explaining its purpose and notifying people that they may be called. Such notice can raise the comfort level and increase the quality of participation. (An example of advance notice of a telephone survey is provided in Figure 6.3.)

FIGURE 6.1   Advance Notice Letter

Dear Customer:

Your business with us is very important. We are always looking for ways in which our products and services can be improved.

You will be receiving a questionnaire from us in the next few days that will address several areas of our organization.

The questionnaire is designed so that you can offer your candid assessment in an anonymous fashion. I sincerely hope that you will find the time to offer us your input.

Thank you for your consideration. I look forward to hearing from you.

Sincerely,

Ernie Entrepreneur
President

FIGURE 6.2   Sample Reminder Postcard

Dear Customer:

This card serves as a gentle reminder concerning a customer questionnaire that we sent to you last week.

If you have already sent the questionnaire back, I sincerely thank you. If you have not yet had an opportunity to complete it, I would encourage you to do so.

Your input is very important to us.

Sincerely,

Ernie Entrepreneur
President

FIGURE 6.3   Advance Notice of a Telephone Survey

Dear Customer:

Your business with us is very important. We are always looking for ways in which our products and services can be improved.

To that end, we have selected customers on a random basis to call and discuss some of the components of our organization over the next ten days.

The questions are designed so that you can offer your candid assessment in an anonymous fashion. Should you be called, I sincerely hope that you will take the time to participate. Your input is very important to us.

Thank you in advance for your consideration. I look forward to hearing from you.

Sincerely,

Ernie Entrepreneur
President

Survey Collection

To facilitate respondent participation, it is important to use data collection methods that are convenient and effective. Here are some collection tips:

- Use a business-reply envelope.
- Provide a closed box for those filling out assessments on-site. It can be uncomfortable for respondents to hand in completed surveys in person. They may feel that the individual collecting the assessments will read the information (e.g., income, age, other preferences, etc.) and immediately associate it with them.
- Provide a reasonable timetable for completion, and state a specific date. Otherwise, the process could go on over an extended period of time.
- Make sure that all of the data comes back to a centralized collection location and is kept there. Otherwise, data can end up in different

places (a secretary's top drawer, the receptionist's desk or in someone's briefcase).

- With telephone surveys, make sure that calls are made at a convenient time for the recipient and that as much sensitivity as possible is used in the conversation so that the data collection process is enhanced.

- If it is an anonymous study, care should be taken to maintain anonymity during the collection process. The respondent should not be identified in any way when the data is received. Do not put names, codes or any other distinguishing characteristics on the data.

- Upon receiving data from respondents, it should be dated and numbered for later tracking, referencing or filing.

Survey Analysis

When planning the analysis component of the research process, remember that *data* is what goes into the analysis process and *usable information* should be what comes out.

In most customer satisfaction research, it is preferable that data be entered into a computer database. The reasons for this recommendation include the following:

- Rapid calculation capabilities (the ability to look at totals, aggregate sums across different variables, different totals, etc.).

- Utilization of different statistical applications.

- A database can serve as a comparative tool for subsequent analyses.

The availability of reasonably priced, high-quality hardware and software make using a database realistic. Depending on your company's requirements, there are many hardware and software applications at several different price levels.

However, you should thoroughly review the information needed before any purchases.

A relevant phrase used in the computer world is "garbage in—garbage out." Regardless of the equipment or software selected, it is imperative that procedures are in place to confirm that data is accurately input into the system.

Sharing Information with Stakeholders

After generating important information pertaining to customer satisfaction, it is necessary to disseminate the information to the relevant parties. An underlying premise regarding this process is that the information has been presented in a readily understandable format.

There are several different groups, or *stakeholders* that have significant interest in your research results. You must establish a process by which the various stakeholders can be adequately briefed.

Management

All members of the management team must be provided with a complete research report so that they may be fully apprised of your firm's performance. The report should include the following:

■ An executive summary in which the parameters of the project are clearly delineated, a summation of the objectives of the project, succinct references to particularly insightful findings and, where appropriate, recommendations for action

■ A table of contents so that topical areas of interest can be readily located

■ Clear presentation of data (easy-to-read tables, summarized statistics, etc.)

■ Clear presentation of the respondent's comments grouped by topic

Employees

When appropriate, employees should be briefed on customer satisfaction findings. This recommendation applies to assessments of your company's performance with customers or employees.

Employees should be fully briefed on what areas need improvement and on those areas where performance is high. Such information enables them to have a realistic understanding of the perceptions held by those dealing with the company. If modifications need to be made, employees can assist in the process.

Customers

In many cases customers are asked for their input, but they never hear the results of the study. It is usually inappropriate for a company to publicly release all information pertaining to a research study because the study may contain confidential data. However, it is likely that there still is much information that can be released.

Releasing *pertinent* information to the public represents a significant marketing opportunity. Upon the completion of a research study, a company can draft a letter to all its customers (unless cost constraints dictate a smaller sample of customers) and provide them a succinct briefing. Such a letter might include the following:

- Thanks to all those who participated
- A restatement of the purpose of the study
- The positive aspects of the findings
- Aspects of the findings that suggest that modifications need to be made to provide better service
- Specific actions being implemented to meet customer concerns

Communicating with customers in this way is an excellent opportunity to reaffirm that their input is important, that your organization is listening to what they have to say and, most importantly, that action is being taken to provide better service.

Do It Yourself or Hire Out?

Is it feasible for a business to conduct a customer satisfaction research project on its own? Certainly. However, each business and its research needs are different and should be evaluated on a case-by-case basis. The requirements of the analysis phase is a key consideration in assessing your company's capability.

Internally Based Research Efforts

To conduct the research internally, someone in the company should be qualified, meaning that the individual (or individuals) has taken research, data analysis and statistics courses or workshops. Without the depth and breadth of a systematic knowledge of research methods, the researcher is inherently limited.

The benefit of conducting an internally based analysis is that you can use existing employees to conduct the project, which is more cost-effective than using an outside firm. The fact that employees know the company and its various products and services, history and culture is an additional benefit associated with using them to conduct their research.

However, there are times when a qualified person may *not* be the ideal person for the task. Such a person may have too many other responsibilities to give the endeavor his or her close supervision.

Ironically, the fact that employees know the company well is also one of the most important reasons *not* to use them to perform customer satisfaction research. They are sometimes too close to the situation to see it objectively. They may also be involved with the politics of the company or may have a vested interest in the outcome of the analysis.

Thus, you should look at each situation before deciding on the person (or persons) to conduct the research.

The Benefits of Using Outside Firms

Even if your company can do the customer satisfaction research internally, you may still wish to consider using an outside firm.

Outside firms are apt to be more objective than employees because they have no personal involvement in the outcome of the research. In addition, due to size and economies of scale, outside firms may be less expensive while also providing considerable expertise.

As stated earlier, each customer satisfaction research project should be evaluated on a case-by-case basis. Here are some important questions to consider:

- Is the project consistent with its stated objectives?
- What is the most effective allocation of resources and employees?
- What is the quality of analysis that will be produced?

Regardless of whether your business decides to conduct its research internally or externally, you must be committed to using the information produced. The chapters that follow provide information on how customer satisfaction research can be used to enhance business performance.

Notes on Using the Assessment

The assessment exercise is not intended to be all-inclusive; each organization and the market in which it operates is unique. The questions raised are intended to help an organization go beyond the facade of "rationalizing" its action or inaction. The assessment tools provided herein are intended to be insightful. It is important that each organization determine the specific relevance of the assessment with respect to its specific situation.

Scoring the Assessment

Filling Out the Form

1. If the statement is generally true of your organization, mark the "yes" column.
2. If the statement is not true of your organization, mark the "no" column.
3. If the statement is occasionally true of your organization, mark the "sometimes" column.
4. If a particular statement does not have relevance to your organization or if information is not available for a credible response, then draw a line through the statement.

Evaluating the Responses

1. A negative answer is seldom favorable. It indicates an absence of a particular activity that may or may not be compensated for elsewhere.
2. A positive answer is almost always favorable. However, too many "yes" answers may indicate that your response is not sufficiently objective.
3. Several "sometimes" answers may point to a lack of direction or commitment.
4. Several "crossed off" questions may indicate insufficient records or an inadequate data base.

Rating the Responses

1. Upon completion of the assessment form, award points as follows:
   - For each "yes" answer, award one point.
   - For each "sometimes" answer, award one-half point.
   - For each "no" answer, award zero points.
   - For each question crossed off the list, award zero points, and deduct one from the total number of questions in the assessment.
2. Divide the total number of points awarded by the number of questions on the assessment (less the number of questions crossed off the list).

$$\text{Score} = \frac{\text{Number of points awarded}}{\text{Number of questions answered}}$$

A score of 1 is excellent. Scores less than 1 should be evaluated with respect to their distance from 1. The farther the score is from 1, the more removed the organization is from initiating actions that are beneficial to superior customer service.

Distribution, Collection and Analysis

Organization: _____ Date: _____ Person Conducting Assessment: _____

	Yes	No	Sometimes
1. In seeking to implement a customer satisfaction assessment, the organization carefully plans survey distribution, collection and analysis.	_____	_____	_____
2. In planning a customer satisfaction assessment, the organization actively plans how results will be shared with different stakeholders (e.g., customers, employees, management, etc.).	_____	_____	_____
3. When sending out a questionnaire by mail, the document is always sent by first-class mail.	_____	_____	_____
4. Whenever appropriate, advance notice is provided to targeted recipients that a questionnaire is coming.	_____	_____	_____
5. When using a mail questionnaire, a reminder postcard is sent.	_____	_____	_____
6. When using a mail questionnaire, a business-reply envelope is included.	_____	_____	_____
7. Respondents are given a firm deadline by which completed responses must be returned.	_____	_____	_____
8. All completed data forms are returned to a centralized collection location.	_____	_____	_____
9. Every effort is made to protect anonymity if the respondents have been told that anonymity is part of the process.	_____	_____	_____

Page total: _____ + _____ + _____ = ☐

	Yes	No	Sometimes

10. Care is taken in the analysis process to ensure that usable information is provided.   _____   _____   _____

11. An effort is made to present assessment findings to stakeholders in a manner that is readily understandable.   _____   _____   _____

12. In communicating relevant findings to stakeholders, an effort is made to outline the actions to be taken to improve customer satisfaction.   _____   _____   _____

13. When deciding whether or not a research project should be done internally, a careful assessment is made as to the qualifications of the personnel slated to do the project.   _____   _____   _____

14. When considering internal or external sourcing of a research project, a careful analysis is done to determine where employees' time could be best spent with respect to revenue enhancement.   _____   _____   _____

15. If an outside firm is used, great care is taken to match the credentials of the firm with the research objectives of the organization.   _____   _____   _____

Page total: _____ + _____ + _____ = ☐

Page 1 Total: = ☐

Page 2 Total: = ☐

Exercise Total: = ☐

7

Are Your Assumptions Correct?

A well-established firm in the Southwest has long prided itself on being one step ahead of market needs. This ability enables it to thwart numerous competitive initiatives to take some of its market share.

However, in recent years the principals of the firm have seemed content with resting on their previous accomplishments. At the same time, the market has grown increasingly competitive.

Mark is hired by the firm to work on running day-to-day operations. Several times during his two-year tenure he has asked to conduct an assessment of core assumptions. However, each time the principals rebuff him, saying that they don't need to spend money gathering information they already know. Ultimately, Mark prevails, which proves fortuitous for the firm.

What Mark's assessment finds is that the firm is no longer considered the leader in any field—whether in price, quality, selection, service, professionalism or location. The assessment also shows that the firm is clearly in a dogfight to preserve market share.

Empowered with such data, Mark awakens the firm from its slumber and restores it as a leader in key competitive areas.

"Our company produces the best widget in the market."

"Our firm provides the most complete turnkey service in the industry."

"Our customers primarily consist of people age 25 to 49 who live within a five-mile radius."

"Our service is the best in the industry."

We hear many of these claims in today's marketplace. But customers must wonder how companies can confirm the validity of such hypothetical statements.

A business may have cause to make these statements for marketing purposes or other reasons. However, it is important that businesses rely on good information for key strategic decisions. They must not rely on rhetoric or traditional assumptions that have not been recently validated. Chapter 2 showed that there can often be a considerable gap between customer expectations and company performance. In this light, it is very important that core organizational assumptions be well understood and frequently validated.

Smaller companies seem to be especially affected by the "tyranny of the urgent." Although they don't have numerous layers of management to deal with, many small companies are simply precluded from assessing key assumptions because their work environments are more hectic. Nonetheless, evaluating key assumptions upon which activity is based is critically important regardless of company size. Some questions to ask regarding key assumptions are as follows:

- What is your company's meaningful point of difference?
- Why does your company offer the products or services it does?
- Why do you select certain channels of distribution to reach particular segments?
- How is your company perceived vis-à-vis the competition?
- Why do customers come to your company rather than going elsewhere?
- Do your employees feel well trained and supported?

In many cases companies are run in adherence to assumptions that are not now relevant to the environment in which they compete. Perhaps the initial target market has undergone transformation, buying preferences have changed, competition has emerged or intensified or the setting in which business is transacted has changed.

Many executives are either unaware of these changes or they simply cannot or will not change core assumptions. Their companies are unable to modify their systems and/or orientation, which ultimately affects product/service delivery and customers' perceptions.

Management by Fact

Upon identifying invalid assumptions, change may be required. Such change may necessitate altering the process by which work is accomplished within the organization. Sometimes change requires new equipment or technology. It may also require realigning management so as to understand the "big picture" of service quality from the customers' point of view. Change almost always requires a willingness to be open to different ways of structuring, measuring and monitoring the way products and services are provided. To bring such change into focus, good customer satisfaction information is required.

Management by fact is an important cornerstone of quality management. Customer satisfaction management is the means by which a business obtains facts. Such information is needed to continuously improve the way a business deals with customers' needs and expectations as well as prospective customers' needs, market perceptions, customer behavior, competitive activity and other external data. This information can come from comment/complaint cards, personal interviews, customer satisfaction measurement surveys or other forms of measurement discussed in Chapter 4.

Choosing a Target Market

A company's target market is crucial to its efforts. There is a range of customer requirements, perceptions and expectations for any product or service in the marketplace. Unless a company custom produces its products or services for each customer, it must optimize its efforts for maximum gain. The company must offer a mix of price, quality and other characteristics to attain a maximum level of customer satisfaction within its target market.

If the target market is not properly identified, a company can find itself hopelessly cornered into trying to be all things to all people. Thus, input from the market should be focused on the company's current target market and any desired target markets. Many companies violate this premise by obtaining input from broad customer groups that include many customers not in the target market. Information obtained this way can corrupt subsequent analysis with extraneous information.

Data from inside the company is also important because it can be useful in managing internal quality. Such data includes manufacturing processes, overhead costs, productivity indices, product cost trends, service processes, cost of quality and employee attitudes.

Innovation and Improvement

The measurement data produced by a company's research efforts serve as significant catalysts for innovation and improvement.

Innovation is important in virtually any business that wants to excel in a competitive environment. Innovation that produces dramatic improvements in service quality, product performance and costing models will give a business an increased competitive advantage. Continuous improvement based on consistent and reliable information from various measurement instruments furthers a firm's competitive position.

Figure 7.1 summarizes a disciplined systematic process that validates critical assumptions throughout the development of products and services.

Goals from the Customer

Companies that have been successful in providing consistently high service quality are known for setting goals to guide their employees. The goals set by these companies usually are based on customers' requirements and expectations derived through customer satisfaction measurements rather than internally driven assumptions.

By not using high-quality external customer satisfaction measurement information to derive and validate assumptions, a company may find itself measuring and monitoring internal standards based on internal assumptions for features and benefits that customers do not care about. At the same time, it may be ignoring other features and benefits that customers do strongly care about.

FIGURE 7.1   A Systematic Process for the Development of New Products or Services

1. Identify customer wants.

2. Determine the market niche.

3. Derive concepts for new product or service.

4. Test concepts against the criteria in steps 1 and 20. Adjust as needed by conducting additional tests with customers or prospective customers.

5. Define product or service specifications that closely reflect customer needs for concepts that pass an initial screening.

6. Test mock-up of specified product or service with customers or potential customers for input.

7. Revise product or service as necessary, and retest with customers and potential customers as required.

8. Devise a detailed marketing program that addresses plans and budgets for sales, sales promotion, advertising, packaging, pricing, distribution and warehousing.

9. Derive a budget based on estimates of costs associated with steps 1–8 and an estimate of sales level.

10. Introduce product or service in the initial targeted areas.

11. Modify marketing plan and forecasted budget based on initial findings from the target area.

12. Roll product or service out full-scale.

Note: The customer or prospective customer plays a critical role in this process. Although no new product or service introduction is free from risk, involving the customer throughout the process reduces the guesswork considerably.

Notes on Using the Assessment

The assessment exercise is not intended to be all-inclusive; each organization and the market in which it operates is unique. The questions raised are intended to help an organization go beyond the facade of "rationalizing" its action or inaction. The assessment tools provided herein are intended to be insightful. It is important that each organization determine the specific relevance of the assessment with respect to its specific situation.

Scoring the Assessment

Filling Out the Form

1. If the statement is generally true of your organization, mark the "yes" column.
2. If the statement is not true of your organization, mark the "no" column.
3. If the statement is occasionally true of your organization, mark the "sometimes" column.
4. If a particular statement does not have relevance to your organization or if information is not available for a credible response, then draw a line through the statement.

Evaluating the Responses

1. A negative answer is seldom favorable. It indicates an absence of a particular activity that may or may not be compensated for elsewhere.
2. A positive answer is almost always favorable. However, too many "yes" answers may indicate that your response is not sufficiently objective.
3. Several "sometimes" answers may point to a lack of direction or commitment.
4. Several "crossed off" questions may indicate insufficient records or an inadequate data base.

Rating the Responses

1. Upon completion of the assessment form, award points as follows:
   - For each "yes" answer, award one point.
   - For each "sometimes" answer, award one-half point.
   - For each "no" answer, award zero points.
   - For each question crossed off the list, award zero points, and deduct one from the total number of questions in the assessment.
2. Divide the total number of points awarded by the number of questions on the assessment (less the number of questions crossed off the list).

$$\text{Score} = \frac{\text{Number of points awarded}}{\text{Number of questions answered}}$$

A score of 1 is excellent. Scores less than 1 should be evaluated with respect to their distance from 1. The farther the score is from 1, the more removed the organization is from initiating actions that are beneficial to superior customer service.

Assessment of Key Organizational Assumptions

Organization: _____   Date: _____   Person Conducting Assessment: _____

	Yes	No	Sometimes
1. The organization has clearly written, concise statements of assumptions upon which its activities are based.	_____	_____	_____
2. Core organizational assumptions are continuously and systematically evaluated and modified in light of market conditions.	_____	_____	_____
3. The organization regularly shares key assumptions with employees for affirmation and/or modification.	_____	_____	_____
4. The organization seeks objective information to support or refute key assumptions on a regular basis.	_____	_____	_____
5. The organization has an objective understanding of what customers perceive to be its strengths and weaknesses.	_____	_____	_____
6. The organization has an objective understanding of why customers purchase its products and/or services.	_____	_____	_____
7. The organization has a clearly defined target market.	_____	_____	_____
8. The organization regularly reviews products and services offered.	_____	_____	_____
9. The organization has an objective understanding of customer expectations.	_____	_____	_____

Page total: ———— **+** ———— **+** ———— **=** ⬜

	Yes	No	Sometimes
10. The organization has objective information pertaining to how it is perceived vis-à-vis the competition.	——	——	——
11. Upon receipt of objective information concerning key organizational assumptions, the organization carefully reviews the information and makes changes where appropriate.	——	——	——
12. The organization shares important information from the marketplace concerning key assumptions with employees.	——	——	——

Page total: —— + —— + —— = ☐

Page 1 Total: = ☐

Page 2 Total: = ☐

Exercise Total: = ☐

8

Employees—
Frontline
Ambassadors

An old-line law firm based in a large midwestern city decides to commission a client satisfaction survey. During one of the briefing meetings with the research firm, the senior partners are asked their thoughts as to the firm's perceived strengths.

Joshua, the managing partner, responds that he feels that the clients will say that the senior partners are a considerable strength of the firm.

When the assessment data is compiled, Joshua is proven correct—to a certain extent. The senior partners are considered the strength of the firm by many clients. However, an even greater number of clients think a secretary/receptionist named Emma is the strength of the firm.

Over the years Emma has endeared herself to clients by doing lots of little things well. She remembers clients by name, asks how family members are doing and makes sure that inquiries are handled promptly. In short, she makes clients feel special.

The tremendously positive impact that Emma has with clients was largely unnoticed by the partners. However, after the assessment results are shared, the partners put Emma in charge of client relations by having her train all of the firm's employees, including partners.

The results have been terrific, as Emma's contributions are significant.

Wat is the the work environment in your firm? Well-constructed business plans and strategies may be lost if you cannot keep good people. Do your managers know their employees' attitudes, feelings, perceptions, product or service knowledge and overall commitment?

Although the internal assessment is important, an external assessment is important as well. What do the company's customers (or potential customers) think about its employees? Are they perceived to be professional, well informed and courteous?

Employees: The Critical Link

Employees are a critical link in any company's endeavors to achieve superior customer satisfaction. It is very difficult to know how employees are feeling about their work. And in most cases, it is probably just as difficult to ascertain what customers and potential customers think about your employees—unless they are asked.

For example, a dentist in the Southwest had a promising practice. The office staff consisted of the dentist, three dental hygienists, a receptionist and a part-time bookkeeper. The dentist worked hard at building his business and had achieved a remarkable level of success in attracting new patients. However, despite long hours and persistence on his part, the practice did not seem to be building its base. For some reason, the dentist wasn't getting many of the first-time visitors to his office to come back.

The dentist decided to commission a patient satisfaction survey and discovered information that helped him understand what was occurring. He and his colleagues got along together well, but his receptionist did not get along well with the patients. Although very pleasant and cordial with co-workers, the receptionist had a tendency to be curt, abrasive and overbearing with patients.

When the problem was identified, the dentist and the receptionist sat down and devised a strategy to remedy the problem areas. The dentist has now built up a large base of steady patients. He summed it up well when he said, "I would not have known had I not asked for input, and I probably would have stayed on the patient replacement treadmill for some time."

Employee Development

A company can have virtually every characteristic required for success except one; and by lacking that one important characteristic, it will in all likelihood fail. A company may be very efficient and may have an experienced staff and sufficient working capital, but it will fail to meet its objectives if it fails to develop its people.

Failure to develop employees can have a significant effect on a company over an extended period of time. Innovative companies recognize the need to contribute to the personal and professional development of their employees. An important objective for any company is to ensure that all employees are encouraged and given the opportunity to develop their personal and professional capabilities through training, education, participation in higher-level management activities and exposure to programs that expand them (e.g., rotation and cross-functional assignments).

Employee Development Must Be Managed

The development of employees should be a carefully planned and managed process. Objectives should be set and a plan carefully followed. In addition, an appropriate budget allocation should be made for the costs required, authority should be clearly assigned, accountability should be clearly understood and standard procedures should be implemented. An important part of this process is making sure that employees receive appropriate orientations upon joining the company. Figure 8.1 provides a suggested checklist for such an orientation.

An important component of any effective employee development program is input from employees regarding their perceptions, frustrations, needs and suggestions. Since employee development is really self-development, employee development efforts should nurture self-confidence and morale. (Figure 8.2 provides suggestions on nurturing self-confidence, while Figure 8.3 provides some relatively straightforward employee enhancement ideas.)

The company only provides the environment and the resources—the employee must do the rest. Thus, for an employee development program to be successful, it is crucial that employee satisfaction be taken into

---

FIGURE 8.1   Employee Orientation Checklist

(The items are listed in no specific order of importance.)

❏ Full information on pay, hours, benefits, policies and procedures, and the terms and conditions of employment is provided.

❏ The responsibilities of each position are clearly explained, and the employee knows to whom to report.

❏ There is ample time to meet other employees and the supervisory staff.

❏ The employee has been given a basic explanation of the organization's history, values, market position and customers.

❏ Written materials have been provided for study, review and reference.

❏ The employee has been given support and ample time to learn and understand the job well.

❏ The employee is brought back in periodically to see if questions have arisen and to assess the transition overall.

❏ The employee is asked to evaluate the orientation effort.

account. (Figure 8.4 shows a sample employee questionnaire, followed by a letter in Figure 8.5, which announces the results of the survey.)

When designing an employee development program, it is also important to get input from customers regarding their experiences with and perceptions of your company's employees. Such input provides an excellent way for management and employees to see how they're perceived by customers. It also provides a common base from which to build a development program.

A Common Beginning

Before the development process begins, employees must know what they will be held responsible for and against what standards their performance will be measured. Otherwise, their efforts may be wasted.

To prevent this from happening, a precise job description must be developed for each employee. The job description should describe the areas or tasks the employee is responsible for, a detailed compilation of performance standards for each task and the behavior expected from the

---

FIGURE 8.2   Nuturing Employee Self-Confidence

Component of Self-Confidence	Ways To Nurture Employee Self-Confidence
Appearance	Tips on dress and grooming
Communication	Coaching, training, role-play opportunities
Goals	Teach and reward goal setting
Health	Encourage well-balanced meals and physical training
High energy level	Stress reduction and exercise programs
Positive attitude	Provide teaching and techniques for developing a positive attitude
Self-esteem	Provide mentors, feedback and recognition

Nurturing employees' self-confidence will help them increase their ability to provide superior customer satisfaction.

---

employee. It is also important that company goals and priorities are clearly explained in the job description.

Such information provides all employees the opportunity to know what is expected not only in their specific assignment, but also for the company as a whole. The company then has a common point of reference—a common beginning—from which measurements can begin. In Figure 8.6 there is a worksheet that can be used to help track employee performance with respect to key customer satisfaction characteristics.

Organizational Attitude

The company should reflect periodically on its attitude toward employee development. The following is a list of questions for companies to consider:

- Has the company instituted policies and procedures that inhibit or discourage "going the extra mile"?

FIGURE 8.3 Employee Enhancement Ideas

Employee-customer relations are largely a reflection of a company's relations with its employees. The list that follows presents some ideas that may be useful to your company. These ideas are shared in no specific order of importance, and some may be more relevant to some businesses than others.

- A collegial work environment encourages an attitude of interdependence and mutual benefit.
- Strong, frequently reinforced values focus on customer satisfaction through superior customer service.
- All levels of management should be easily accessible.
- Companies should have periodic assessment surveys of employee attitudes.
- Companies should have periodic customer satisfaction surveys, with the results shared with employees.
- Managers are seen as coaches and counselors, rather than as judges or critics.
- Companies should provide merit pay.
- Promote from within when possible.
- Provide periodic reviews that include candid, bilateral discussions of a performance appraisal and feedback to improve performance.
- Provide exit interviews for all employees who leave.
- Facilitate open communication, including a company newsletter.
- Provide paid employee referral programs.
- Provide employee-driven benefit packages.
- Provide educational assistance.
- Provide annual physicals for employees and their spouses.
- Give public recognition and rewards for jobs well done.
- Institute a liberal leave policy for use in family or special emergencies.
- Plan employee/family gatherings away from the work environment that are sponsored in whole or in part by the company.
- Encourage an employee input/suggest program with incentives.
- Hold periodic open group discussions between management and employees on how to improve both the work environment and customer service.

FIGURE 8.4 Sample Employee Questionnaire

Dear Employee:

Enclosed is a brief questionnaire that asks a series of questions concerning your expectations and perceptions of the firm.

Please take a few minutes and fill it out. Your input is very important to us.

Your responses will be kept completely confidential as anonymity will be maintained.

A summary of results will be published in the quarterly newsletter. Thank you in advance for your participation.

Sincerely,

John Q. Executive

---

1. What do you consider to be Acme's greatest strength in terms of treatment of employees?

   _____
   _____
   _____

2. What do you consider to be Acme's greatest weakness in terms of treatment of employees?

   _____
   _____
   _____

3. What do you consider to be Acme's greatest strength in the market vis-à-vis the competition?

   _____
   _____
   _____

4. What do you consider to be Acme's greatest weakness in the market vis-à-vis the competition?

   _____
   _____
   _____

5. Who do you consider to be Acme's competition?

   _____
   _____

   Why? _____
   _____

FIGURE 8.4　Sample Employee Questionnaire　(continued)

6. Please rate the health-care coverage provided by Acme.
   ❏ Excellent　　　　❏ Good　　　　　❏ Average　　　　❏ Poor
   Why do you say that?_____

   _____

7. Please rate the quality of supervision you receive in your present position.
   ❏ Excellent　　　　❏ Good　　　　　❏ Average　　　　❏ Poor

8. Please rate your perception of the morale of employees at Acme.
   ❏ Excellent　　　　❏ Good　　　　　❏ Average　　　　❏ Poor

9. How satisfied are you with your job with respect to the kind of work you do?
   ❏ Very satisfied　　　　❏ Somewhat satisfied　　　❏ Indifferent
   ❏ Somewhat dissatisfied　　❏ Very dissatisfied

10. Please rate the quality of training provided to you for your present position.
    ❏ Excellent　　　　❏ Good　　　　　❏ Average　　　　❏ Poor

11. If you were to make two suggestions to improve Acme with respect to its relationship with employees, what would they be?
    1. _____
    2. _____

12. If you were to make two suggestions to improve Acme with respect to its competitive position in the market, what would they be?
    1. _____
    2. _____

Thank you for your input.
It is greatly appreciated.

FIGURE 8.5 Sample Letter to Employees

Dear Employees:

To all of you who participated in the recent assessment program, I would like to offer my sincere thanks.

As expected, there were numerous ideas and suggestions that, when implemented, will have an immediate impact on the firm.

I would like to share with you several highlights of the study.

- Result A
- Result B   (*Cite results that were particularly positive.*)
- Result C, etc.

However, there were several other results that clearly show we have several areas we need to work on. Such information provides us an opportunity to improve our company. Some of these items are as follows:

- Suggestion/Input A
- Suggestion/Input B
- Suggestion/Input C, etc.

- Planned Action A
- Planned Action B
- Planned Action C, etc.

Thank you for your participation and input. Together we can pursue excellence in every component of our organization.

Sincerely,

President

Note: Using a feature in a company newsletter to share ideas and suggestions is also effective.

- Has the company provided the sufficient support, supervision and resources that enable employees to succeed?
- Are employees proud to work for the company?
- Do employees have suggestions for improvement, and is the company receptive to receiving such input?
- Does the company provide employees with the proper incentives for achieving superior performance and excellent customer service, or do employees feel taken for granted?

FIGURE 8.6   Employee Assessment of Customer Satisfaction Characteristics

Instructions

This worksheet is designed to be a comparative tool to assess performance levels across important characteristics. The characteristics identified in this figure are for illustrative purposes only. When utilizing the worksheet, select characteristics that are specifically relevant to your organization's unique set of circumstances.

For accuracy of comparison, use a similar survey instrument (if not the exact same kind) as an assessment tool each time you use the worksheet.

Terminology:

Date 1:   This refers to the first assessment date. Dates 2, 3 and 4 refer to subsequent assessment dates.

Difference: To obtain this number, subtract the earlier date from the most recent date. For example, in this figure Date 1 would be subtracted from Date 2, and the difference would be recorded in the difference column to the right of Date 2. Date 2 would be subtracted from Date 3, and the difference would be recorded in the next difference column, and so forth. Note that a positive sign in the difference column indicates an improving trend, while a negative sign implies a downward trend.

- What can the company do to keep employees happy?

The best way to know is to ask. Your employees are the best consultants you could ever have. They are very well qualified to assess your company, and they know what is right and wrong within the organiz tion.

The Cost of Quality

Developing quality employees brings tremendous reward to a business, its management and the customers (who receive better service as a result). But it also has a price. Part of the price is the expense of organizing, training, staffing and supporting a group of employees that understands the business, its customers, competitors, and products and services.

FIGURE 8.6 Employee Assessment of Customer Satisfaction Characteristics (continued)

Components of Customer Satisfaction	Date 1	Date 2	Difference	Date 3	Difference	Date 4	Difference
Appearance							
Product knowledge							
Professionalism							
Problem-solving skills							
Returns phone calls							
Order follow-through							
Frequency of contact							
Courtesy							
Punctuality							

Difference = present score – previous score.

Scoring: Excellent = 4.0   Average = 2.0
           Good = 3.0   Poor = 1.0

Note: Any negative scores in the difference columns should be carefully reviewed.

Another part of the price is the cost of listening to customers and employees consistently. This requires a willingness to ask questions, to be vulnerable and to act upon the input received.

The price of leadership also involves periodically reviewing and evaluating employees, analyzing employees' strengths and weaknesses candidly and objectively and setting up improvement programs that will help employees be more productive by developing their full capabilities in a supportive and nurturing environment. Ideally, a company can improve and develop competitive strategies that are innovative and workable.

In such a setting, all parties "win," and employee satisfaction helps to produce high levels of customer satisfaction.

Notes on Using the Assessment

The assessment exercise is not intended to be all-inclusive; each organization and the market in which it operates is unique. The questions raised are intended to help an organization go beyond the facade of "rationalizing" its action or inaction. The assessment tools provided herein are intended to be insightful. It is important that each organization determine the specific relevance of the assessment with respect to its specific situation.

Scoring the Assessment

Filling Out the Form

1. If the statement is generally true of your organization, mark the "yes" column.
2. If the statement is not true of your organization, mark the "no" column.
3. If the statement is occasionally true of your organization, mark the "sometimes" column.
4. If a particular statement does not have relevance to your organization or if information is not available for a credible response, then draw a line through the statement.

Evaluating the Responses

1. A negative answer is seldom favorable. It indicates an absence of a particular activity that may or may not be compensated for elsewhere.
2. A positive answer is almost always favorable. However, too many "yes" answers may indicate that your response is not sufficiently objective.
3. Several "sometimes" answers may point to a lack of direction or commitment.
4. Several "crossed off" questions may indicate insufficient records or an inadequate data base.

Rating the Responses

1. Upon completion of the assessment form, award points as follows:
   - For each "yes" answer, award one point.
   - For each "sometimes" answer, award one-half point.
   - For each "no" answer, award zero points.
   - For each question crossed off the list, award zero points, and deduct one from the total number of questions in the assessment.
2. Divide the total number of points awarded by the number of questions on the assessment (less the number of questions crossed off the list).

$$\text{Score} = \frac{\text{Number of points awarded}}{\text{Number of questions answered}}$$

A score of 1 is excellent. Scores less than 1 should be evaluated with respect to their distance from 1. The farther the score is from 1, the more removed the organization is from initiating actions that are beneficial to superior customer service.

Employee Assessment

Organization: _____ Date: _____ Person Conducting Assessment: _____

	Yes	No	Sometimes
1. The personal and professional development of employees is recognized as a vital activity.	———	———	———
2. Internal training and retraining sessions are held on a regular basis.	———	———	———
3. The organization measures customer satisfaction with respect to employee performance on a regular basis.	———	———	———
4. The organization measures employee satisfaction on a regular basis.	———	———	———
5. The effectiveness of the organization's employee development is measured and evaluated regularly.	———	———	———
6. The organization diligently works at encouraging employee development.	———	———	———
7. The organization actively seeks input from employees on improving the quality of work life.	———	———	———
8. Developmental needs are discussed on a regular basis with employees.	———	———	———
9. The performance and potential of each employee is reviewed on a periodic basis with a superior.	———	———	———
10. Employee's have clear job descriptions for which they are held accountable.	———	———	———

Page total: ——— + ——— + ——— = ☐

	Yes	No	Sometimes
11. Employees feel like they are an important part of the organization.	————	————	————
12. Employees feel they are properly recognized and given incentives for providing superior customer service.	————	————	————

Page total: ———— **+** ———— **+** ———— **=** ☐

Page 1 Total: **=** ☐

Page 2 Total: **=** ☐

Exercise Total: **=** ☐

9

How Do You Keep Your Customers?

Jim has an impressive resumé. He received excellent training while employed as a brand manager for a Fortune 500 company. For two years now, he has been running a small sales-driven company in the Northeast.

Because of his experience working in a large company, Jim proves relentless in his admonitions to employees to attract more customers. Those admonitions are carefully heeded, as the firm records more new customers in Jim's two years than ever before in its history.

However, the firm has not shown any measurable increase in revenues or profits during Jim's tenure. A customer satisfaction assessment reveals that existing customers feel that the firm's objective is to get new customers. But consequently, existing customers don't feel well taken care of, and many are compelled to leave.

When he receives this data, Jim immediately changes the focus of the firm, realizing that the perpetual pursuit of new customers without keeping a majority of them has proven ineffective.

Within nine months of refocusing the firm, the number of new customers is not as high as before. However, the number of customers staying with the firm has risen markedly, as have monthly revenues and profits.

FIGURE 9.1   Cost of Losing Customers

Information required:

(A)   =   Number of customers
lost. (Choose the
appropriate time period
for your firm—monthly,
quarterly, biannually or
annually.)

    _____

(B)   =   Average revenue per
customer. (You can divide
an annual figure to get
the amount equivalent to
the time period selected.)

$ _____

(C)   =   Profit margin. (This figure
should be derived as a
function of the revenue
figure.)

_____ %

(D)   =   Administrative costs—
amount to open
accounts, amount to
close accounts

+$ _____

(E)   =   Estimated marketing cost
per customer (cost
associated with securing
the customer)

$ _____

Calculation—Financial Cost

_____ (A)

× $ _____ (B)

= $ _____ Lost annual revenue

× _____ % (C)

= $ _____ X _____ Profit lost

$ _____ (D)

× _____ (A)

= $ _____ Y _____

X+Y = Financial impact of lost customers

FIGURE 9.1   Cost of Losing Customers (continued)

Calculation—Marketing Cost

$\$$ _____(E)

$\times$ _____$\$$

$= \$$ _____X_1_____Marketing expense lost

Assumption of having to replace lost customers requires the firm to repeat:

$\$$ _____(E)

$\times$ _____(A) Number of customers lost = number of customers to regain.)

$= \$$ _____X_2_____Market expense lost

$X_1 + X_2$ = Marketing cost of lost customers

Customer retention is one of the most important strategic issues companies face in the 1990s. Retention is critical for increasing profits and remaining competitive. Studies show that a 5 percent change in the rate of customer retention can shift profits from 25 percent to 100 percent in either direction.

In manufacturing, measuring the number of defects is an important index of quality. In measuring service, the number of *defections* (customers going elsewhere) is important.

Many companies significantly underestimate the cost of customer defections. Very few companies track defections (otherwise known as *migration*) or invest in reducing them. (A worksheet that will help you calculate the cost of losing customers is provided in Figure 9.1.)

Companies should measure customer migration, and their goal should be customer retention. They must regularly evaluate and modify training programs, information systems, organizational structure, complaint handling procedures, hiring objectives, incentives and even the company culture. A strategy of customer retention will produce extraordinary results, because customers will beat a path to the company that provides superior customer service.

The High Cost of Migration

Failure to realize the high cost of losing customers stems in part from aggressive selling and marketing. In many companies, the work involved in keeping customers is seen as dull and tedious. Selling is what is truly exciting. Many companies view unhappy customers as chronic complainers who are not worth the effort required to satisfy them.

It is true that some customers are habitual complainers, but too often companies apply this label to every customer who complains. If this attitude permeates a company, a dissatisfied customer will probably receive poor treatment and his or her problems will remain unaddressed.

Prospective and first-time customers usually are treated well during the selling courtship. Many companies aggressively pursue new customers, but these customers go right out the door if service is poor. They come in with great expectations but leave with disappointment, frustration and possibly resentment.

Marketing: A Two-Part Process

The marketing function should be viewed as a two-part process of (1) getting customers and (2) retaining customers.

The first part of the marketing process rarely has inadequate resources and seldom suffers from a lack of attention. Sales budgets, advertising campaigns and promotional efforts usually take a significant percentage of a company's operating budget. However, retention marketing often has little or no budget at all. Depending on the specific industry, research shows that it costs between five and seven times as much to get a new customer as it does to keep an existing one.

Most companies have little difficulty defending the significant costs of acquiring new customers. But what if the new customers are only replacements for dissatisfied customers? Such companies find themselves barely holding on to customers, or worse yet, they experience a net loss of customers.

Companies that do engage in efforts to retain customers have returns policies, customer complaint departments and occasional customer mailings. But few companies engage in aggressive, well-constructed strategies of retention-oriented marketing that keep customers happy and mend relations with dissatisfied customers.

The Moment of Truth

Every point of contact a customer has with a company—whether by phone, in person or by mail—is a point of service delivery. It is a time when the customer forms one more impression and makes one more judgment about the company. Some call it the "moment of truth." Nordstrom's, a department store, operates by the following maxim: "Listen to the customer; the customer is always right. Do anything to satisfy the customer."

Every time a company fails to live up to a promise to its customers, it loses some credibility.

Advertising, public relations, architectural design and other high-profile efforts may create favorable impressions. But the critical difference in customer retention usually occurs in less glamorous areas. For example, customers may be impressed by the behavior and appearance of employees, the way the phones are answered, the clarity and accuracy of billings or the overall promptness and reliability in handling complaints.

The little things are important, and companies must be vigilant and consistent in their attention to detail. This may require redefining the role of marketing, rearranging priorities and reallocating budgets.

Obstacles to Superior Customer Service

There are several obstacles to customer service that at one time or another affect most businesses.

The Attitude That Customers Are Replaceable

The days of monopolistic enterprises and taking customers for granted have long since passed away. Customers are considered to be valuable assets obtained through hard work and considerable expense. However, employees are often relieved when disgruntled customers leave, which is an unfortunate attitude for any employee or business to have.

Companies should never act as if they have exclusive domain over their customers or as if there is a limitless supply of new customers.

Insensitive Managers

The old expression "no two people are alike" applies to both employees and customers. Problems develop when managers become insensitive to the characteristics or behavior of their employees and customers. Managing the human element is a considerable challenge in providing superior customer service.

Managers must continuously respond to changing situations. They must be able to make moment-to-moment decisions in an environment where education, experience, skills, perceptions, values and prejudices have a direct impact on transactions with employees and customers. In addition, other concerns—such as a divorce, financial trouble or sick children—will affect employee-customer transactions.

Given these human idiosyncrasies, companies must monitor, train, motivate, evaluate and periodically retrain employees so that they are empowered to be of assistance to customers.

Budgetary Problems

Some companies do not properly fund customer-service enhancement efforts. As a result, they end up with inconsistent customer-service strategies and poor implementation.

In a highly competitive economy, budgetary constraints can drive away frustrated customers who are told, for example, that there aren't enough qualified people, or there aren't enough people to catch up on back orders. And in many companies, the financial resources required to meet customer needs exist, but they are being allocated elsewhere. Insufficient funding inherently devalues the importance of customer service in the minds of frontline employees.

Lack of Strong Commitment

In many cases, management doesn't have a strong commitment to superior customer service. They may claim to have a strong commitment, but in reality they only give customer service "lip service." Unless management undertakes a full-scale effort and requires an intense commitment to superior customer service throughout the organization, the prospects of achieving superior customer service are seriously diminished.

Inconsistency

Customers usually measure a product or service by the satisfaction they expect and subsequently receive. If a customer is sold a product or service that doesn't live up its promises, dissatisfaction occurs. Customers who are oversold or promised undeliverable levels of satisfaction usually forget the salesperson and concentrate on the product or service involved and the company behind it.

Thus, companies must strive for consistency in the areas of product and service delivery, representation of product and service characteristics and employee professionalism.

Lack of Listening

Managers, who are typically concerned with the big picture, seldom have time to get out and really listen. Many managers are comfortable believing that if customers are not complaining, things must be going all right. This is a dangerous assumption.

Managers must be available to employees and customers. They must observe and listen purposefully and systematically. Most importantly, they must be open to discussion and should not be apprehensive about being proved incorrect.

Inertia

Computer systems, policy guides and procedures often take on a life of their own in many companies. Customers are frustrated when told "I'm sorry, but our policy is . . ." or "There is nothing that I can do about it." In some companies, the computer systems are handy excuses for mistakes.

Although computer systems, policies and procedures are important, if not kept in check, they can stifle a company's primary mission—to sell and service customers. Companies that excel in providing superior customer service focus on the customer and strive diligently not to allow "the system" to interfere with what is best for the customer.

Different Frames of Reference

There are many words frequently used to describe customer service. Such words include *prompt, reliable, satisfaction, courtesy, professional, timely,* and *quality* as well as phrases such as "quick response to customer complaints," "accuracy in billing," "prompt repairs" and "satisfaction guaranteed."

For these words to have relevance, there must be specific definitions, measurements or other explicitly stated standards. For example, "quick response to customer complaints" can be defined to mean within 24 hours. "Accuracy in billing" can mean that if errors are identified within seven days of receipt, a correction will be made. With such definitions clearly understood from the start, your company and its customers will have a common denominator by which to measure the quality of service provided.

Lack of Perspective

Providing high-quality customer service is not the type of program that can be bought and paid for in a short period of time. High-quality customer service cannot be effectively implemented and sustained with memos, short-lived promotional efforts or advertising campaigns designed to boost sales.

Management must view high-quality customer service as an ongoing process. The "tyranny of the urgent" often prevents managers from taking steps that will help keep the customers the company worked so hard to get.

How To Increase Customer Retention

The previous section looked at nine frequently encountered obstacles that prevent companies from providing superior customer service. This section examines several suggestions that will help your company successfully retain as many of your customers as possible.

Reliability

Customers want consistent performance most of all. To be reliable, your company needs to strive for the following:

- Do what you say you are going to do.
- Do it when you say you are going to do it.
- Do it right the first time.

Credibility

Customers will go back to businesses that want to help them and have their best interests in mind. Customers don't want hidden agendas, fine print, hard-sell tactics or extra charges. They want the products or services they buy to be free of danger, risk and doubt.

Responsiveness

We live in a time of instant gratification. When customers want service, they usually want it immediately. Being responsive requires being available, accessible and willing to help customers whenever they have a problem.

Empathy

Being empathetic means putting yourself in the position of your customer. Would you do business with your company? Every customer is unique and wants to be treated uniquely. To accomplish this, your company must ask the right questions, listen intently and then design a product or service to meet the stated needs.

Select Frontline Employees Carefully

Companies oriented toward customer service should have customer-friendly people in frontline positions. Such positions are not for everybody. Great care should be exercised in selecting prospective employees based on their personality traits and other skills. A psychological consulting firm has singled out the following attributes as especially helpful for employees in frontline positions:

- An ability to make sound judgments in a stressful setting
- A problem-solving orientation
- A desire to be liked
- A naturally optimistic outlook

Companies should empower employees to provide the best possible service they can. When selecting frontline personnel, give them sufficient authority with which to do their jobs efficiently. For example, customers and employees are often frustrated when simple transactions have to be approved by supervisors. This causes employees to feel inadequate and customers to wait.

Provide Sufficient Employee Training

Customers want to be served by knowledgeable employees. Thus, employees should be well trained before interacting with customers.

Employee training should not be viewed as a one-time entrance requirement. Regular training sessions are needed to keep employees updated on new policies and procedures, new product features and benefits, competition, customer needs, new programs, developments in other parts of the company and core corporate goals.

Create a Sense of Belonging

Employees also need a sense of their company's mission and their role within the company. They need to receive encouragement to enhance their roles while also receiving recognition for contributions made. Regardless of the methods used by different companies, employee recognition is an important motivator and a fundamental tool for nurturing an environment committed to customer service.

Avoid the Premature Release of Products, Concepts or Policies

Taking a new product or service to market before it is ready, changing policies rapidly or introducing a new computer system before all the bugs are worked out erode customer satisfaction levels. Companies must take great care not to sacrifice customers while trying to achieve progress. Customers want consistency and stability.

Make Things Easy for the Customer

Making things easy for the customer requires careful planning, coordination and persistent diligence. When companies don't work at these fundamentals, customer service can be seriously impaired.

The following are ways in which you can make things easier for your customers:

- Install a toll-free number.
- Make sure you have enough incoming phone lines.
- Hire enough employees to quickly answer phones.
- Use business-reply mail (postage-paid).
- Make sure to have easy refund and exchange procedures.
- Provide prompt and accurate information.
- Don't assume that the customers have extensive product or service knowledge.
- Speak and write in plain English; don't use highly technical terms or company jargon.
- Debrief defectors.

If a Customer Leaves, Ask Why

Whenever your company loses a customer, find out why the customer left. There are few customers who will be more honest or candid than a dissatisfied customer. (A sample lost-customer inquiry and questionnaire is provided in Figure 9.2.)

FIGURE 9.2   Sample Inquiry and Questionnaire for Lost Customers

Inquiry

Dear Customer:

Our primary goal is to provide our customers the best products and services possible. Therefore, we are always concerned when a customer stops doing business with us.

I would like to know about your experiences with our firm. I would greatly appreciate it if you would take a few minutes to answer the questions enclosed. Your input is very important to us as we seek ways in which we can provide better products and service. Your response will be kept confidential.

A postage-paid envelope has been enclosed for your convenience.

Thank you in advance for your assistance. I hope we may have the privilege of serving you again in the future.

Sincerely,

President

Questionnaire

1. How long have you been a customer with_____?

2. What products/services did you buy from_____?

3. Please indicate the reason (or reasons) why you have ceased doing business with _____. (Please check all that apply.)

Moved from	Products/services offered no longer
❏ area	❏ needed

Service provided	Personnel	Took my business to
❏	❏	❏ another firm

❏ Firm made errors on account (Please specify.)
_____

4. Have you placed your business with another firm?

   ❏ Yes   ❏ No

   If yes, with whom?_____

5. If you were to make one suggestion to _____, to improve its operation, what would it be?
_____

6. Age (different options)

7. Income (different options)

   Thank you for your input. It is greatly appreciated.

Notes on Using the Assessment

The assessment exercise is not intended to be all-inclusive; each organization and the market in which it operates is unique. The questions raised are intended to help an organization go beyond the facade of "rationalizing" its action or inaction. The assessment tools provided herein are intended to be insightful. It is important that each organization determine the specific relevance of the assessment with respect to its specific situation.

Scoring the Assessment

Filling Out the Form

1. If the statement is generally true of your organization, mark the "yes" column.
2. If the statement is not true of your organization, mark the "no" column.
3. If the statement is occasionally true of your organization, mark the "sometimes" column.
4. If a particular statement does not have relevance to your organization or if information is not available for a credible response, then draw a line through the statement.

Evaluating the Responses

1. A negative answer is seldom favorable. It indicates an absence of a particular activity that may or may not be compensated for elsewhere.
2. A positive answer is almost always favorable. However, too many "yes" answers may indicate that your response is not sufficiently objective.
3. Several "sometimes" answers may point to a lack of direction or commitment.
4. Several "crossed off" questions may indicate insufficient records or an inadequate data base.

Rating the Responses

1. Upon completion of the assessment form, award points as follows:
   - For each "yes" answer, award one point.
   - For each "sometimes" answer, award one-half point.
   - For each "no" answer, award zero points.
   - For each question crossed off the list, award zero points, and deduct one from the total number of questions in the assessment.
2. Divide the total number of points awarded by the number of questions on the assessment (less the number of questions crossed off the list).

$$\text{Score} = \frac{\text{Number of points awarded}}{\text{Number of questions answered}}$$

A score of 1 is excellent. Scores less than 1 should be evaluated with respect to their distance from 1. The farther the score is from 1, the more removed the organization is from initiating actions that are beneficial to superior customer service.

Customer Retention Assessment

Organization: _____ Date: _____ Person Conducting Assessment: _____

	Yes	No	Sometimes
1. The organization has an ongoing employee-training program.	———	———	———
2. The organization treats every customer as a prized possession that is not expendable.	———	———	———
3. The organization supports the pursuit of superior customer service through sufficient budget allocations.	———	———	———
4. The organization works diligently to keep its promises.	———	———	———
5. Management has a strong commitment to customer service.	———	———	———
6. The organization holds employees to high levels of performance and appearance.	———	———	———
7. The organization carefully defines elements of customer-service measurements to ensure "same language" communication.	———	———	———
8. Management diligently checks to see that policies, procedures and protocol do not stifle customer service.	———	———	———
9. Management has a long-term commitment to providing superior customer service.	———	———	———
10. The organization carefully selects employees who represent its commitment to superior customer service.	———	———	———

Page total: ——— + ——— + ——— = ☐

		Yes	No	Sometimes
11.	The organization works diligently to make each employee feel he or she belongs.	_____	_____	_____
12.	The organization has a strong commitment to continuous training.	_____	_____	_____
13.	The organization is careful not to release new products or services unless they are well tested.	_____	_____	_____
14.	The organization regularly informs employees about what is going on elsewhere in the organization.	_____	_____	_____
15.	Management grants frontline employees sufficient authority to enable them to promptly resolve customer problems.	_____	_____	_____
16.	The organization has a strong commitment to making everything as easy and convenient for the customer as possible.	_____	_____	_____
17.	The organization has a strong commitment to resolving complaints as soon as possible.	_____	_____	_____
18.	Management treats complaints or problems as opportunities for the company to improve.	_____	_____	_____
19.	The organization has a commitment to doing whatever it takes to get the job done right the first time.	_____	_____	_____
20.	Management teaches employees that each customer should be perceived as a long-term investment.	_____	_____	_____
21.	Management fosters an environment in which employees feel comfortable sharing ideas that may enhance customer service.	_____	_____	_____

Page total: _____ + _____ + _____ = ☐

	Yes	No	Sometimes
22. Management has a strong commitment to consistency.	————	————	————
23. The organization seeks to regularly assess how it compares to the competition.	————	————	————
24. The organization has a strong commitment to taking care of details.	————	————	————
25. Management periodically assesses its commitment to providing superior customer service.	————	————	————

Page total: ———— + ———— + ———— = ☐

Page 1 Total: = ☐

Page 2 Total: = ☐

Page 3 Total: = ☐

Exercise Total: = ☐

CHAPTER

10

How Customers Can Help You Beat the Competition

Every year Susan travels the annual industry trade-show circuit in hopes of finding the hot new products or services for the coming year. She and her staff fan out on "reconnaissance" missions in pursuit of what will be most effective in the marketplace. In some years Susan even retains the services of a consultant.

But no matter what strategy she uses, her efforts meet with mixed results. Growing weary of the effort and expense involved, Susan contemplates an alternative methodology. She decides to modify the customer satisfaction measurement instruments to include a thorough inquiry into what customers identify as significant trends or hot new products or services.

Susan finds this new methodology to be a very effective way of accurately identifying new opportunities at a greatly reduced cost.

Any business should see itself not as a goods-producing or service-producing company but rather as one committed to customer satisfaction. A company begins with customers and their needs—not with a unique product, patent or new service. In essence, companies should work in reverse: they should first focus on the delivery of customer satisfaction and then move back to creating the goods or services through which satisfaction is attained.

The Purpose of Business

According to Peter Drucker, the purpose of business is to create and keep customers. Companies should constantly seek to offer better or preferred products or services through the different combination of means, places and prices so that customers prefer to do business with them. Since preferences are always being shaped and reshaped, companies need a favorable proportion of targeted customers to purchase their products or services.

Customers usually do not buy "things"; they buy tools to solve problems or meet needs. Companies that know their customers' problems are more likely to be successful in helping to provide the solutions than those who only know the equipment. An undifferentiated product or service becomes differentiated when the "offered" product or service makes a difference in getting customers. The "delivered" product or service is key in keeping them.

Product Life Cycle

Most products and services conform to a pattern or process called the life cycle. The life cycle progresses through the following stages: market development, market growth and market decline.

In the life-cycle process, the market-development stage is the most challenging. To know how a company's product or service is faring with the customer or how a competitor's offering is faring, there must be regular communication with the customers. When a company develops a new product or service, it should plan at the outset a series of steps to be taken at various stages so that information will be readily available to help management plan action that will enable the company to sustain sales and profit for as long as possible.

If your product or service successfully passes the market-development stage, competitors may imitate the success. They may even come out with product improvements and lower prices.

Many companies operate under the premise that they must be innovative if they are to survive, let alone grow. Consequently, considerable resources are often committed to the pursuit of new, innovative products and services. To avoid this disproportionate allocation of your resources, explore the competitive environment in which your company operates. Remember that the customer is the critical component in your assessment.

When considering a major commitment, ask yourself the following questions:

- How does a policy of innovation compare to more modest objectives?
- Can the pursuit of innovation be promising based on developments to date?
- Put in the context of a vigorous cost-benefit analysis, are existing efforts justifiable?

Innovation or Imitation

Innovation can be viewed from two perspectives:

1. Something that has never been done before
2. Something that has not been done before by the industry or company now doing it

When other companies in the same industry copy a new product or service, it is not innovation. Even if it is something new for them, it is *imitation*.

Research and development can be very time-consuming, costly and frustrating to those waiting for output. The development process requires an enormous commitment of people and capital—with no assurances of an acceptable return on investment. However, when a company focuses its efforts on trying to adapt to things that have been done successfully elsewhere, the development effort becomes quite different. Thus, you should determine what your target market wants and then develop that product or service in ways your competitors do not: In other words, work back from what other companies have done.

In most sectors of the economy, any company that is not diligently aware of innovative possibilities may be taking a significant competitive risk. For a company to be market oriented, it must seek innovation, where appropriate, in the areas of new services, new products, product features and benefits and customer service. Therefore, your company must have a balanced orientation in the pursuit of innovation vis-à-vis imitation. More importantly, no company can afford to try to be first in everything.

Creativity, commitment and management capabilities usually are too evenly distributed within industries, and the costs are too great.

At the beginning of a new-product process, one innovator usually is followed by numerous imitators. A basic premise of marketing is that a business should determine what customers need and want and then vigorously work to satisfy those needs and wants provided that:

- doing so is consistent with the organization's strategy; and
- the forecasted rate of return meets company objectives.

The following are core assumptions of business development efforts:

- A customer is best defined by a complete marketing program (product, information, distribution, price, promotion, customer service, etc.) rather than just the product itself.
- Different customers will need and want different things.

Importance of Timing

The faster the speed with which new products are introduced, the more critical the need for each business in that economic sector to derive a concise strategy that serves not only to guide business decisions but also to influence research and development commitments. In many sectors of the economy, the survival and growth of individual companies requires that they quickly imitate the innovator's new products or services. Since the speed of competitive imitation has a tendency to quickly reduce the margins available to all participants, the timing with which an imitator enters the market is critical.

While many companies do a careful and detailed job in planning new product or service innovations, few have any criteria for what is a bigger and more important job—new product imitation. What have customers approved or accepted elsewhere? Many companies don't have policies—formal or informal—to guide their reactions to the innovations of others. Timely customer information helps companies with limited resources target their efforts more efficiently.

Differentiation

A product or service seldom has a competitive position in and of itself; somehow it must become differentiated. Customers assign value to products and services in direct proportion to the ability of those products or services to help meet their needs. Whatever a product or service is in terms of its ability to attract and satisfy customers can be managed. However, it seldom is. Once a customer is sold, he or she can be easily unsold if expectations are not fulfilled.

In some cases customers may be unaware of when they are being served well. (This is especially true in the area of intangible products and or services.) Customers may not know or appreciate what they are getting until it is not received. This can be dangerous for a business because it may mean that customers are only aware of dissatisfaction, not of success or satisfaction. They may then be particularly susceptible to the claims of competitors. (Such claims are less likely to have an effect if a company has conducted customer satisfaction assessments and communicated the results back to its customer base, as described in Chapter 2.)

Decision-Making Priorities

Good information about the market, customers and competitors can help a company move in the right direction. Such information can stimulate the process of creating new products and services.

A product has to be created before it can be chosen. Work well done in the pursuit of "wrong" products and services can be more damaging to a company than work poorly done in the pursuit of the "right" products and services.

Companies must have systematic plans for building sales. Information for sales building can come from those in the distribution channel. This enables a company to position itself to make things happen rather than finding itself having to react to things that are already happening. If a company tries to do too many things at once, most of which tend to be reactive, it will do few of them well.

Companies should make *market intelligence* (the process of gathering information on the market) an active, exciting and participatory

---

FIGURE 10.1   Sample Employee Participation Card

MARKET TIP

A "great" example of:

❑ Great customer service   ❑ new product   ❑ new service

An "exciting" idea for:

❑ Great customer service   ❑ new product   ❑ new service

Where:_____

What:_____

Who: _____

When: _____

How: _____

Comments: _____

Submitted by: _____

The ongoing input received from a wide cross-section of respondents with a considerable range of perspectives can serve as an outstanding source of information that will help your company compete favorably. Market intelligence is a valuable tool in an incessantly changing, competitive environment.

---

activity for all employees. The card in Figure 10.1 can be passed out to employees and dropped off at a designated place.

When possible companies should reward employee participation. Rewards can include cash bonuses, public recognition or promotions, depending on the magnitude of the input.

Notes on Using the Assessment

The assessment exercise is not intended to be all-inclusive; each organization and the market in which it operates is unique. The questions raised are intended to help an organization go beyond the facade of "rationalizing" its action or inaction. The assessment tools provided herein are intended to be insightful. It is important that each organization determine the specific relevance of the assessment with respect to its specific situation.

Scoring the Assessment

Filling Out the Form

1. If the statement is generally true of your organization, mark the "yes" column.
2. If the statement is not true of your organization, mark the "no" column.
3. If the statement is occasionally true of your organization, mark the "sometimes" column.
4. If a particular statement does not have relevance to your organization or if information is not available for a credible response, then draw a line through the statement.

Evaluating the Responses

1. A negative answer is seldom favorable. It indicates an absence of a particular activity that may or may not be compensated for elsewhere.
2. A positive answer is almost always favorable. However, too many "yes" answers may indicate that your response is not sufficiently objective.
3. Several "sometimes" answers may point to a lack of direction or commitment.
4. Several "crossed off" questions may indicate insufficient records or an inadequate data base.

Rating the Responses

1. Upon completion of the assessment form, award points as follows:
   - For each "yes" answer, award one point.
   - For each "sometimes" answer, award one-half point.
   - For each "no" answer, award zero points.
   - For each question crossed off the list, award zero points, and deduct one from the total number of questions in the assessment.
2. Divide the total number of points awarded by the number of questions on the assessment (less the number of questions crossed off the list).

$$\text{Score} = \frac{\text{Number of points awarded}}{\text{Number of questions answered}}$$

A score of 1 is excellent. Scores less than 1 should be evaluated with respect to their distance from 1. The farther the score is from 1, the more removed the organization is from initiating actions that are beneficial to superior customer service.

Marketing Reconnaissance

Organization: _____ Date: _____ Person Conducting Assessment: _____

	Yes	No	Sometimes
1. The organization pursues objective information about its present and prospective customers (e.g., interests, needs, buying habits, preferences.	_____	_____	_____
2. The organization diligently reviews objective information about its present and prospective customers and modifies its behavior as required.	_____	_____	_____
3. The organization pursues objective information about competitors with respect to their strengths and weaknesses, products, services and sales methods and strategies.	_____	_____	_____
4. The organization diligently reviews the objective information about its competitors to assess its ability to compete effectively.	_____	_____	_____
5. The organization regularly assesses its selling efforts to determine their effectiveness in the marketplace vis-à-vis competitors.	_____	_____	_____
6. The organization periodically assesses market demand.	_____	_____	_____
7. The organization actively assesses key influences that affect the sale of its products or services.	_____	_____	_____
8. The organization has a clearly defined set of objectives concerning innovation of new products or services.	_____	_____	_____

Page total: _____ + _____ + _____ = ☐

	Yes	No	Sometimes

9. The organization actively monitors new product or service introductions in sectors in where it competes.

10. The organization systematically evaluates new product or service introductions to assess their impact on its own product or service offerings.

11. Shifts in market demand are regularly monitored throughout the new-product development process so that changes in direction and timing can be made.

12. The organization has methods whereby field personnel can regularly submit new product/service ideas.

Page total: _____ + _____ + _____ = ⬜

Page 1 Total: = ⬜

Page 2 Total: = ⬜

Exercise Total: = ⬜

11

How Effective Are Your Marketing Efforts?

George and his wife Kathy have owned a printing business in Florida for six years. As part of a national franchising organization, they are consistently recognized for excellent performance in annual growth vis-à-vis their peer group nationwide.

Thus, when asked about their marketing efforts, they offer their six-year record as proof of the effectiveness of their efforts (which consist largely of print and radio advertising).

George and Kathy decide to measure their marketing as a component of an assessment of customer satisfaction. After conducting a survey of customer-based data, they find that a majority of their customers learn of the firm by word of mouth "just passing by." Although some of their customers acknowledge the impact of the print and radio advertising, it is a small minority.

Thus, what George and Kathy assumed to be a primary driver of their growth was actually shown to be incidental. With this knowledge, they decide to reduce their expenditures in print and radio advertising and bolster their efforts elsewhere.

Do your company's products or services have a clearly defined point of difference? If so, does it come through in your promotional efforts?

Is your company under great pressure to move its products or services? If so, selling is probably considered more important than marketing. The difference between the two is that *selling* emphasizes the needs of the seller, and *marketing* emphasizes the needs of the buyer. Selling focuses on the seller's desire to convert product into cash; marketing focuses on the need to satisfy customers through products and all that is associated with creating, delivering and consuming them.

Marketing efforts are often measured for their effectiveness by sales revenue, market share and profitability. Although these measures are important, they do not go far enough. It is also important to measure the methods used, the emphases given, the objectives pursued and the overall impact on the customer. An ongoing evaluation of marketing and promotion efforts aids in the pursuit of objectives and keeps a company from succumbing to periodic aberrations in the economy. Maintaining such a focus helps a company adhere to the key aspects of its overall strategy.

Advertising and promotion activity must be focused on accomplishing objectives that are consistent with the strategies and policies that are the foundations of the organization. In addition, companies must have an unwavering commitment to treating customers and potential customers with utmost respect and sensitivity when seeking to persuade them to buy their products or services.

Define Your Message

Potential customers are rarely able to make direct comparisons between your product or service and the products or services offered by competitors. In most instances, they can only compare your advertising and promotional efforts with the efforts of competitors. If your company's assertions are deemed more credible and persuasive, customers may choose your product or service. And if the product or service lives up to the representations made, the customers are satisfied. However, if the product's performance fails to deliver adequately, your company may lose customers permanently.

A company must determine what are its key messages and whether those messages are getting out effectively through its advertising campaigns and promotional efforts. This can be done through assessing the impact of the messages on customers through a satisfaction-based survey. And remember, key messages should be regularly and convincingly reinforced.

Target Your Customer

When a company creates advertising and promotional campaigns that depict its product or service, they should accurately portray what customers will actually experience. Products and services are at risk of failure when a company consistently exaggerates quality and is unable to deliver the product or level of service depicted in advertising or promotional efforts. To avoid such an occurrence, thorough coordination and communication between the advertising and promotion departments and product and service providers is essential.

How do your company's advertising and promotional campaigns affect the next stage of the product life cycle? Do they place the product or service into an untenable position? Are they annoying or offensive to the target market? Research has shown that a significant source of dissatisfaction with advertising comes from the difference between the people for whom specific products, brands, messages and services are intended and the people who are exposed to them.

Prepare Your People

It is not uncommon in many companies to run advertising or launch promotional campaigns before informing employees. In many instances, advertising or promotional efforts promise particular services or benefits to customers before employees are brought up to speed. Customers responding to advertisements or promotions come to employees to ask questions about the advertised products and services. And if uninformed, employees feel frustrated, ill-prepared and even helpless.

You can avoid this scenario by briefing employees on forthcoming campaigns and seeking input from frontline personnel prior to launching campaigns. When they are given the opportunity to preview advertising and/or promotional campaigns, employees will be better prepared for the customers. Superior customer service can therefore be delivered when the advertising and promotion departments communicate regularly with operations personnel.

Measuring Marketing Effectiveness

Assessing your company's marketing and promotion activities is critical to growth and survival, since most companies are dependent on the success of these efforts. It is important to determine if marketing and promotional efforts contribute to your company's success and if so, how. It is rare to find marketing or promotion that is so good that it cannot be improved.

An assessment of marketing and promotion is helpful in guiding management to efficiently allocate resources to those areas with the greatest opportunity or the greatest need. It helps to identify relative strengths and weaknesses by putting them in proper perspective. Many executives expend considerable effort supervising and/or performing many marketing-related tasks. But seldom is such intensity directed toward determining how well these tasks are performed. Without such an evaluation, a company may not know why some programs are effective and others are not.

Promise and Deliver

First-time customers carefully scrutinize a company's product or service. If they are persuaded to buy a product or service by inflated, false or misleading claims, they may never buy from that company again. And if evaluation methods are not in place, the company may never know why their customers defected.

Advertising and promotional efforts must be based on an accurate representation of the product or service, its features and benefits, market characteristics, competitive considerations and a sensitivity to the impact on potential customers.

Notes on Using the Assessment

The assessment exercise is not intended to be all-inclusive; each organization and the market in which it operates is unique. The questions raised are intended to help an organization go beyond the facade of "rationalizing" its action or inaction. The assessment tools provided herein are intended to be insightful. It is important that each organization determine the specific relevance of the assessment with respect to its specific situation.

Scoring the Assessment

Filling Out the Form

1. If the statement is generally true of your organization, mark the "yes" column.
2. If the statement is not true of your organization, mark the "no" column.
3. If the statement is occasionally true of your organization, mark the "sometimes" column.
4. If a particular statement does not have relevance to your organization or if information is not available for a credible response, then draw a line through the statement.

Evaluating the Responses

1. A negative answer is seldom favorable. It indicates an absence of a particular activity that may or may not be compensated for elsewhere.
2. A positive answer is almost always favorable. However, too many "yes" answers may indicate that your response is not sufficiently objective.
3. Several "sometimes" answers may point to a lack of direction or commitment.
4. Several "crossed off" questions may indicate insufficient records or an inadequate data base.

Rating the Responses

1. Upon completion of the assessment form, award points as follows:
   - For each "yes" answer, award one point.
   - For each "sometimes" answer, award one-half point.
   - For each "no" answer, award zero points.
   - For each question crossed off the list, award zero points, and deduct one from the total number of questions in the assessment.
2. Divide the total number of points awarded by the number of questions on the assessment (less the number of questions crossed off the list).

$$\text{Score} = \frac{\text{Number of points awarded}}{\text{Number of questions answered}}$$

A score of 1 is excellent. Scores less than 1 should be evaluated with respect to their distance from 1. The farther the score is from 1, the more removed the organization is from initiating actions that are beneficial to superior customer service.

Assessment of Marketing Efforts

Organization: _____   Date: _____   Person Conducting Assessment: _____

	Yes	No	Sometimes
1. The organization periodically assesses interest, utilization and awareness levels of its products and/or services.	_____	_____	_____
2. The organization establishes threshold levels of revenue or profit a product or service must generate to be kept in its portfolio.	_____	_____	_____
3. The organization periodically assesses products or services customers want.	_____	_____	_____
4. The organization regularly assesses competitive strategies regarding resource allocation.	_____	_____	_____
5. Changes in the competitive environment are monitored throughout the new product/new service development process so that changes in timing and direction can be made as needed.	_____	_____	_____
6. Management consistently uses strategic competitive analysis to assess the viability of products and services.	_____	_____	_____
7. Review of resource allocation is specifically assigned and carefully monitored.	_____	_____	_____
8. The organization has a specific budget allocation for strategic competitive assessment of resource allocation.	_____	_____	_____

Page total: _____ + _____ + _____ = ☐

	Yes	No	Sometimes
9. Competitive evaluations regularly and promptly detect significant competitive developments with respect to resource allocation strategies.	————	————	————
10. The effectiveness of resource allocation reviews is periodically measured and evaluated.	————	————	————
11. The organization actively participates in seeking key information that illustrates important trends with respect to resource allocation.	————	————	————
12. Management actively seeks input with respect to maximizing the return on invested capital.	————	————	————

Page total: ———— + ———— + ———— = ☐

Page 1 Total: = ☐

Page 2 Total: = ☐

Exercise Total: = ☐

12

Do You Say What You Mean To Say?

Sondra is a perfectionist. In all that she does, she strives for excellence and expects the same of the employees in her regionally based sales organization.

Needless to say, Sondra is dismayed when, at a sales gathering, several customers vocalize their dissatisfaction with the correspondence received from the firm.

The letter one customer received in response to a billing discrepancy was curt and inaccurate. In another case, a customer received a letter from one of the sales representatives that had numerous typographical errors and poor grammar. And yet another customer complained of poor phone skills.

While acknowledging her commitment to excellence, many of Sondra's customers find that the firm's communication efforts are less than excellent. Thus, she wonders what other customers might think if not familiar with her commitment to excellence.

Do your company's customer communications convey an impression of a well-run, professional organization? Do customers feel that their interests and needs are known, listened to and addressed?

Customer communication is a pervasive activity that either directly or indirectly involves every member of a firm. It begins when you make the first contact with a prospective customer, and it continues indefinitely.

Customer communications include some of the following activities:

- Responding to customer or potential customer inquiries
- Prospecting for new customers
- Quoting prices and product availability
- Keeping customers informed about the status of their orders
- Keeping sales personnel informed concerning the availability of products or services
- Acknowledging and handling complaints
- Explaining service and return policies
- Resolving billing errors
- Customer follow-up
- Measuring customer satisfaction
- Sales calls

In essence, customer communications involve virtually any contact with a customer.

And each contact should encourage the customer or prospective customer to want to do business with the firm.

Personalize Your Communications

Every effort should be made to personalize customer communications. Through data base management programs and mail-merge capabilities, which have been available for several years and have dropped considerably in price, even the smallest companies have access to high-quality, customized communication.

In some circumstances, a handwritten note may be appropriate and may even mean more to a customer. However, if you send handwritten notes, be sure that the form of correspondence is consistent with your company's image and that there are no spelling or grammatical errors.

The telephone is another way to establish personal communication, but too often it is not used effectively. Secretaries may inquire as to who is calling, but when the boss comes to the phone, he or she never uses the name provided. Or you may have conversations with company representatives who do not identify themselves, are hard to understand or are ill-informed and unable to help you satisfy the need for which the call was made in the first place.

Here are some questions to ask concerning your customer communications:

- What is the quality of communications that emanate from your company?
- Is your letterhead crisp and professional?
- Are letters well written and easy to read?
- Has care been taken to ensure that there are no misspellings?
- Is the phone answered in a pleasant and professional manner?
- Are communications skills valued and nurtured by management?

As has been discussed throughout this book, the only sure way to know how your company is perceived by customers is to ask them directly and measure their satisfaction and perceptions.

Good Customer Communications Start with Management

Effective customer communications begin in a firm's executive office. So often the attitudes and behavior of employees are really a reflection of management priorities. If management sincerely believes that the customer (and potential customer) is important and reinforces this commitment through quality communication at all levels, employees will treat customers with consideration and respect—whether it be in person or through written or telephone communications.

Good customer communications require a strong financial commitment. To present a high-quality, professional image, an effective communications program requires central direction, control and measurement of performance—all of which involve considerable financial resources. Efforts at creating and maintaining high-quality communications produce myriad benefits. Otherwise, the consequences can be disastrous.

Virtually all of us have received mass-produced form letters; billing statements that are hard to read and difficult to understand; correspondence that is not customized; and phone service that lacks professionalism, courtesy and competence. Every one of those contacts with

---

FIGURE 12.1   Telephone Communication Checklist

Date:_____   Employee:_____   Reviewer:_____

❑ Phone answered within _____ rings
❑ Proper greeting
❑ Proper organization identification
❑ Proper personal identification
❑ Clear speaking/easy to understand
❑ Proper inquiry—how the caller can be helped
❑ Efficient transfer of call (if appropriate)
❑ Accurate transfer of call (if appropriate)
❑ Professionalism
❑ Careful monitoring of "hold" process (if applicable)

Comments: _____

_____

_____

---

customers (and potential customers) creates an impression in the mind of the recipient that is not easily displaced.

Customer communications should be monitored periodically. Unless this is done, the quality of communication will deteriorate, and management will be unaware of the problem until the complaint file builds or customers migrate elsewhere. Three simple checklists are provided in Figures 12.1, 12.2 and 12.3 to help your company monitor its employee communications.

International Communications

With an increasingly global economy, more companies are doing business internationally. When communicating across borders, make sure that your message is clearly understood and that the customer (or potential customer) is not offended in the process. Complicated words or phrases may confuse people from other countries, various words or

---

FIGURE 12.2   In-Person Communication Checklist

Date:_____   Employee:_____   Reviewer:_____

- ❑ Nicely groomed
- ❑ Proper greeting
- ❑ Promptness in greeting customer
- ❑ Proper personal identification
- ❑ Proper inquiry as to how the customer can be served
- ❑ Good product/service knowledge
- ❑ Good selling of product/service
- ❑ Good selling of organization
- ❑ Professionalism
- ❑ Good control of conversation

Comments:_____

_____

_____

---

references may offend them and some words may have a far different connotative meaning than what is intended.

A basic understanding of the country with which you are doing business and a sensitivity to its culture will minimize communications problems. Another safeguard that can be used to avert poor communication is to have a person familiar with the targeted country review all communication prior to dissemination.

Communications Assistance

In most cases, employees want to be good communicators. However, for one reason or another, some may feel intimidated or ill at ease. To help employees overcome these problems, your company can provide assistance. Such assistance is described in the following sections.

FIGURE 12.3   Written Communication Checklist

Date:_____   Employee:_____   Reviewer:_____

❑ Strict adherence to organizational image parameters
❑ Clarity of writing
❑ Customization of correspondence
❑ No misspellings
❑ Professional presentation
❑ Conveys personal competency

   Conveys organizational competency (i.e. no
❑ misrepresentations)
❑ Conveys knowledge
❑ Contains a "call to action"
❑ Gramatically correct

Comments: _____
_____
_____
_____

FIGURE 12.4   Sample Telephone Script

Good (morning, afternoon, evening). Acme Foods. This is Susan. How may I help you?

(Inquire how the call may be directed if the targeted individual is not available, personally intervene and take the message and see to it that the message is promptly forwarded.)

(Prior to forwarding the call, or prior to hanging up after taking a message . . .)

Thank you for calling Acme Foods, Mr. _____ or Mrs. _____ (if name was given).

FIGURE 12.5   Order Confirmation

ACME Company
123 Research Drive
Anytown, AZ 12345-6789
(607)789-5432

Dear_____: (Personalize.)

Thank you very much for your order. This note is to confirm that the following items:

- Item A
- Item B
- Item C
- Item D

will be shipped by _____, 199__. Should you have any questions concerning this order, please feel free to call me toll-free at 1-800-222-2222. Thank you for giving us the opportunity to serve you.

Sincerely,

Ernie Entrepreneur

Applications: Sales people (that sold to the customer so that they can follow the process through to completion)

Shipping departments (so they can take responsibility and have pride in the shipping function)

Telephone Communications

Management can provide a written script or outline for employees to read, study and refer to during telephone calls. This will provide a comfort level for the employees from which they can build, and it removes the "guesswork." The script or outline contains the framework of what an employee should say—a greeting, the company name, the employee name and an inquiry as to where the employee can direct the call. As employees grow more comfortable with their roles, confidence

---

FIGURE 12.6 Complaint Call Response

ACME Company
123 Research Drive
Anytown, AZ 12345-6789
(607)789-5432

Dear_____: (Personalize.)

Thank you for taking time to call in on _____. I appreciate your bringing the problem to our attention. That type of input helps our company do a better job.

Should you have any further difficulty, please feel free to call me toll-free at 1-800-222-2222.

Sincerely,

Ernie Entrepreneur

Applications: Customer-service agents
                 Salespeople
                 Receptionists
                 Management

In-Person Communications

Managers may want to provide role-play training to impart specific knowledge and experience to employees. They can also coach employees by participating with them in in-person encounters. This helps nurture their confidence and comfort level in meeting customer needs.

FIGURE 12.7 Potential Customer Visit

ACME Company
123 Research Drive
Anytown, AZ 12345-6789
(607)789-5432

Dear_____: (Personalize.)

Thank you for taking time to stop in on _____ (actual day). I enjoyed visiting with you. I hope that we may have the privilege of serving you in the near future. Should you have any questions about our products or services, please do not hesitate to call on me at 222-2222.

Sincerely,

Ernie Entrepreneur

Applications: Sales clerks
                Store managers
                Receptionists
                Sales associates

Written Communications

The area of written communications is seldom given enough attention in customer communications. However, many employees say written communication is one of the most intimidating components of interacting with customers.

Written communication is considered by most companies as highly repetitive in nature. But it requires customization and personalization in its specific application to customers and potential customers.

Thus, a company may want to create a sample correspondence manual that provides a framework for the numerous letters constituting the bulk of its written correspondence. This might include letters concerning prospecting, sales, shipping, receivables or collection. Employees could then draw upon this resource and customize the letters as appropriate. (Figures 12.5, 12.6 and 12.7 are examples of letters covering common situations.) A correspondence manual can save employees several hours of drafting time while also assuring management that their employees are producing high-quality correspondence. And if the letters are loaded in a computer data base, employees will only have to make the necessary modifications and send the letters to the printer.

Conclusion

Ensuring that your company is known for the quality of its communication, regardless of the particular type, is a commitment that can yield significant benefits for your company immediately as well as over the long term.

Notes on Using the Assessment

The assessment exercise is not intended to be all-inclusive; each organization and the market in which it operates is unique. The questions raised are intended to help an organization go beyond the facade of "rationalizing" its action or inaction. The assessment tools provided herein are intended to be insightful. It is important that each organization determine the specific relevance of the assessment with respect to its specific situation.

Scoring the Assessment

Filling Out the Form

1. If the statement is generally true of your organization, mark the "yes" column.
2. If the statement is not true of your organization, mark the "no" column.
3. If the statement is occasionally true of your organization, mark the "sometimes" column.
4. If a particular statement does not have relevance to your organization or if information is not available for a credible response, then draw a line through the statement.

Evaluating the Responses

1. A negative answer is seldom favorable. It indicates an absence of a particular activity that may or may not be compensated for elsewhere.
2. A positive answer is almost always favorable. However, too many "yes" answers may indicate that your response is not sufficiently objective.
3. Several "sometimes" answers may point to a lack of direction or commitment.
4. Several "crossed off" questions may indicate insufficient records or an inadequate data base.

Rating the Responses

1. Upon completion of the assessment form, award points as follows:
   - For each "yes" answer, award one point.
   - For each "sometimes" answer, award one-half point.
   - For each "no" answer, award zero points.
   - For each question crossed off the list, award zero points, and deduct one from the total number of questions in the assessment.
2. Divide the total number of points awarded by the number of questions on the assessment (less the number of questions crossed off the list).

$$\textbf{Score} = \frac{\text{Number of points awarded}}{\text{Number of questions answered}}$$

A score of 1 is excellent. Scores less than 1 should be evaluated with respect to their distance from 1. The farther the score is from 1, the more removed the organization is from initiating actions that are beneficial to superior customer service.

Communications Assessment

Organization: _____ Date: _____ Person Conducting Assessment: _____

	Yes	No	Sometimes
1. The organization has well-defined image parameters (e.g., stationery design, consistent logo, color, type, font, size, etc.).	————	————	————
2. Quality customer communication is recognized as a vital activity that is strongly endorsed by management.	————	————	————
3. The actions and behavior of employees that communicate with customers by telephone, in person or in writing are guided by written procedures.	————	————	————
4. All employees who communicate directly or indirectly with customers by telephone, in person or in writing are thoroughly trained with respect to attitude, conduct and professional courtesy.	————	————	————
5. All employees communicating with customers by telephone, in person or in writing identify themselves and provide a number by which they can readily be reached should customers have follow-up questions at a later date.	————	————	————
6. Customer communications are directed through the appropriate salesperson; or, at a minimum, they are copied and the appropriate person is informed as to the disposition of the communication.	————	————	————

Page total: ———— + ———— + ———— = ☐

	Yes	No	Sometimes
7. Customer billing statements have a knowledgeable contact person identified and a phone number where the individual can be easily reached.	_____	_____	_____
8. The organization provides numerous examples of quality communication to employees for them to use as references.	_____	_____	_____
9. The organization encourages employees to frequently communicate with customers.	_____	_____	_____
10. Management periodically visits with employees regarding communications efforts and seeks input.	_____	_____	_____
11. The handling of customer communications is audited on a random basis to ensure that they conform with organizational goals and objectives.	_____	_____	_____
12. The effectiveness of customer communications is evaluated periodically.	_____	_____	_____
13. The organization maintains a phone log of incoming customer calls to track the types of calls received.	_____	_____	_____
14. The logs are periodically reviewed by management to improve performance in customer service.	_____	_____	_____
15. Management periodically calls in from the outside to evaluate the phone-handling skills of employees.	_____	_____	_____

Page total: _____ + _____ + _____ = ☐

Page 1 Total: =   ☐

Page 2 Total: =   ☐

Exercise Total: =   ☐

13

Benchmarking: How Do You Measure Up?

Richard is a national sales manager for a firm based in the Southwest. He has long been a proponent of the importance of providing superior customer service as a cornerstone in building a successful sales organization.

Richard requires his sales professionals to attend customer-service seminars regularly and provides them with a steady stream of reading materials. However, over a three-year period, he is only able to discern a marginal increase in customer satisfaction ratings for the firm.

Richard decided to have the customer satisfaction assessment instrument modified so that responses can be tracked by sales region. Upon receipt of the initial data, he then has a starting point from which subsequent performance periods can be compared. The areas of comparison included several components of customer satisfaction (e.g., product knowledge, professionalism, frequency of contact, etc.).

This method of tracking and use of comparative data is incorporated into the compensation bonus review process. In 18 months, the firm's ratings in customer satisfaction rise dramatically.

*W*ebster's Dictionary defines *benchmark* as "a point of reference from which measurements may be made." Within the context of a business, *benchmarking* refers to analyses of customers, competitors, trends in the market, differences in product or service attributes and company performance.

Benchmarks offer an opportunity to achieve substantial improvement by adopting or adapting ideas. They help encourage creativity through an exposure to performance measures and alternative approaches and results. Properly derived, benchmarks challenge companies to beat the best—internally or externally. Thus, they encourage major improvements rather than the fine tuning of existing methods or procedures.

David Kearns, former CEO of Xerox, has stated that benchmarking is "the continuous process of measuring products, services and practices against the toughest competitors, or those companies recognized as industry leaders." He has also said that benchmarking is a critically important process to implement, regardless of the size of an organization.

Benchmarking is an important component in any management effort to increase customer satisfaction through strategic quality management. It involves developing a set of performance measurements that are regularly updated and incorporated into a company's planning and review efforts. With this information, managers can evaluate the improvements made in customer satisfaction. If quality improvements do not meet planned goals, the reasons for the shortfall can then be specifically examined.

The following are three basic components of benchmarking:

1.   Competitive benchmarking
2.   Premier benchmarking
3.   Internal benchmarking

Each of these components will be discussed in this chapter. However, first it is important to note that to be effective and relevant, benchmarking depends on consistent and reliable objective customer satisfaction information.

Competitive Benchmarking

Competitive benchmarking compares a company's performance with respect to the customers' perceptions of superior customer service and satisfaction against either the best in the industry or direct competitors, whichever is more appropriate.

Competitive Benchmarking Assessments

When conducting a competitive benchmarking assessment, the following five factors should be considered.

1. The company must diligently determine what customers think quality customer service means. It is important that this is determined by objective customer input versus internal assumptions.

2. The company may need to develop a formalized policy of innovative imitation if competitors are found to be better in areas that are critical to providing superior customer service and satisfaction.

3. The company may need to create a new complement of value-added products or modified services that have a different focus or require additional employee training.

4. The company may need to modify its advertising and promotional efforts if it is determined that key quality and service attributes are not getting out and are not known by customers or potential customers.

5. The company may find unique niches or particular segments of a market that are responsive to a grouping of product or service characteristics the company provides.

Obtaining Competitive Benchmarking Information

Many of the methods discussed in Chapter 4 (e.g., written surveys, telephone interviews, focus groups, interviews) can be effective in obtaining objective customer-based input that can be used in a benchmarking assessment. Whichever method is chosen, the data collection process must be consistent and equitable. In other words, each respondent must have the opportunity to respond to characteristics of a competitive company.

A chart is provided in Figure 13.1 to help you evaluate your performance with respect to other companies. The chart is designed so that information generated from a satisfaction assessment survey can be inserted into the chart and used for comparative purposes.

FIGURE 13.1 Competitive Benchmarking Worksheet

Instructions

This chart utilizes numerical values that have been derived in a survey to assess customer satisfaction levels across defined characteristics among comparative organizations.

The letters refer to the selected comparative organizations.

Numerical values from the completed survey analysis that equate to the legend at the bottom of the chart should be inserted into the respective squares.

The best score among comparative organizations should be determined for each characteristic and placed in the best-score column.

The organization score in a given characteristic should be placed in the next column.

The difference column is derived by subtracting the first column from the organization's score column.

The average score column is derived by adding all of the comparative scores in a characteristic row and dividing by the number of comparative organizations.

The second difference column is derived by subtracting the average score value from the organization's score column.

A negative value in either of the difference columns is an indication that better customer satisfaction is being generated at an organization other than the theoretical organization in the respective service characteristic.

A chart that has already been filled out is provided in Figure 13.2. Note that in the first difference column, the sample company ties with the best of the comparative companies in timeliness, competence and selection. However, the sample company scores below the best of the comparative companies in courtesy, professionalism, product knowledge, problem-solving skills, attitude, prices, quality and phone-answering skills. In the second difference column, the sample company shows superior performance in timeliness, competence and selection; ties the average in courtesy; and scores less than the average in professionalism, product knowledge, attitude, prices, quality and phone-answering skills.

FIGURE 13.1 Competitive Benchmarking Worksheet (continued)

Date: _____   Reviewer: _____

Characteristics	Comparative Organizations					(1) Best score among compet-itors	(2) Organi-zation score	Differ-ence (2–1)	(3) Average score	(2) Organi-zation score	Differ-ence (2–3)
	A	B	C	D	E						
Courtesy											
Professionalism											
Timeliness											
Product knowledge											
Competence											
Problem-solving skills											
Attitude											
Prices											
Quality											
Selection											
Phone-answering skills											

Scoring: Excellent = 4.0   Good = 3.0   Average = 2.0   Poor = 1.0   Don't know = no score

Any negative scores in either difference column should be carefully reviewed by assessing what skills, systems or programs the higher-scoring organization has that yours does not have or does differently than yours does and why.

FIGURE 13.2   Sample Competitive Benchmarking Worksheet

Date: _____   Reviewer: _____ *Sample* _____

Characteristics	Comparative Organizations					(1) Best score among compet- itors	(2) Organi- zation score	Differ- ence (2–1)	(3) Average score	(2) Organi- zation score	Differ- ence (2–3)
	A	B	C	D	E						
Courtesy	4	3	3	2.5	2.5	4	3	-1	3	3	0
Professionalism	4	3	3.5	4	3.5	4	3	-1	3.7	3	-.7
Timeliness	2.5	3	2.5	4	3	4	4	0	3	4	+1
Product knowledge	4	3	3	3	4	4	3	-1	3.5	3	-.5
Competence	4	3	3.5	3.5	3	4	4	0	3.5	4	+.5
Problem-solving skills	3	3	2	4	3	4	3	-1	3	3	0
Attitude	4	4	3	3	3	4	3	-1	3.5	3	-.5
Prices	2	3	4	3	4	4	3	-1	3.3	3	-.3
Quality	3	3	3	4	4	4	3	-1	3.5	3	-.5
Selection	3	3	4	3	4	4	4	0	3.5	4	+.5
Phone-answering skills	4	4	3	3.5	3.5	4	3	-1	3.7	3	-.7

Scoring: Excellent = 4.0   Good = 3.0   Average = 2.0   Poor = 1.0   Don't know = no score

Any negative scores in either difference column should be carefully reviewed by assessing what skills, systems or programs the higher-scoring organization has that yours does not have or does differently than yours does and why.

You can prepare a chart on a regularly scheduled basis and compare it against previously prepared charts to assess performance gains or losses. But remember that the characteristics and number of competitive companies selected in Figures 13.1 and 13.2 are for illustrative purposes only. Your company may want to assess different characteristics across a different number of companies.

When in possession of the kind of information these charts provide, a company can know how it is performing vis-à-vis in comparative companies in key areas that affect customer satisfaction.

Premier Benchmarking

Premier benchmarking is studying or reviewing the "top of the class" in a specific customer-service area. Such an assessment involves going outside a company's own industry to learn new ways of improving customer service and satisfaction. Companies can improve internal functions that affect customer satisfaction by innovatively imitating "star" companies outside their industry.

A format that is helpful in using premier benchmarking is provided in Figures 13.3, 13.4, 13.5 and 13.6. The characteristics related to customer service in these figures have been selected for illustrative purposes. (For example, in Figure 13.3, professionalism is assessed; in Figure 13.4, frequency of contact; in Figure 13.5, overall customer satisfaction; and in Figure 13.6, shipping/delivery.) You will want to select characteristics that have specific relevance to your company.

FIGURE 13.3   Premier Benchmarking Assessment—Professionalism

Date:_____   Reviewer:_____

Objective:	To identify the premier organization that embodies "top of the class" performance in the identified characteristic. The premier organization may be found outside the industry in which this organization competes.
Implementation note:	The organization should select key customer-service characteristics throughout the year to assess. There should be strict accountability for someone in management to specifically follow through on the status of recommendations.

Characteristic	**Premier Organization**	**Key quality service/satisfaction attributes exemplified by the premium organization**
		_____
		_____
Professionalism	_____	_____
		_____
		_____
		_____

Source(s) of information: _____

_____

Recommendation(s): _____

_____

_____

_____

_____

_____

FIGURE 13.4   Premier Benchmarking Assessment—Frequency of Contact

Date:_____   Reviewer:_____

Objective: To identify the premier organization that embodies "top of the class" performance in the identified characteristic. The premier organization may be found outside the industry in which this organization competes.

Implementation note: The organization should select key customer-service characteristics throughout the year to assess. There should be strict accountability for someone in management to specifically follow through on the status of recommendations.

Characteristic	Premier Organization	Key quality service/satisfaction attributes exemplified by the premium organization
		_____
		_____
Frequency of Contact	_____	_____
		_____
		_____
		_____

Source(s) of information: _____

_____

Recommendation(s): _____

_____

_____

_____

_____

_____

FIGURE 13.5   Premier Benchmarking Assessment—Overall Customer Satisfaction

Date:_____   Reviewer:_____

Objective: To identify the premier organization that embodies "top of the class" performance in the identified characteristic. The premier organization may be found outside the industry in which this organization competes.

Implementation note: The organization should select key customer-service characteristics throughout the year to assess. There should be strict accountability for someone in management to specifically follow through on the status of recommendations.

Characteristic	**Premier Organization**	**Key quality service/satisfaction attributes exemplified by the premium organization**
		_____
		_____
Overall Customer Satisfaction	_____	_____
		_____
		_____
		_____

Source(s) of information: _____

_____

Recommendation(s): _____

_____

_____

_____

_____

_____

FIGURE 13.6   Premier Benchmarking Assessment—Shipping/Delivery

---

Date:_____   Reviewer:_____

Objective: To identify the premier organization that embodies "top of the class" performance in the identified characteristic. The premier organization may be found outside the industry in which this organization competes.

Implementation note: The organization should select key customer-service characteristics throughout the year to assess. There should be strict accountability for someone in management to specifically follow through on the status of recommendations.

Characteristic	**Premier Organization**	Key quality service/satisfaction attributes exemplified by the premium organization
		_____
		_____
Shipping/Delivery	_____	_____
		_____
		_____
		_____

Source(s) of information: _____

_____

Recommendation(s): _____

_____

_____

_____

_____

_____

FIGURE 13.7   Internal Benchmarking Worksheet

Instructions

This worksheet is designed to be a comparative tool to assess performance levels across important characteristics. The characteristics identified in this figure are for illustrative purposes only. When utilizing the worksheet, select characteristics that are specifically relevant to your organization's unique set of circumstances.

For accuracy of comparison, use a similar survey instrument (if not the exact same kind) as an assessment tool each time you use the worksheet.

Terminology:

Date 1:   This refers to the first assessment date. Dates 2, 3 and 4 refer to subsequent assessment dates.

Difference: To obtain this number, subtract the earlier date from the most recent date. For example, in this figure Date 1 would be subtracted from Date 2, and the difference would be recorded in the difference column to the right of Date 2. Date 2 would be subtracted from Date 3, and the difference would be recorded in the next difference column, and so forth. Note that a positive sign in the difference column, indicates an improving trend, while a negative sign implies a downward trend of some.

Internal Benchmarking

Internal benchmarking is the internal measurement of improvements in customer satisfaction over time. The measurement can involve individual efforts, company-wide efforts; and measurements between other offices, facilities, plants, divisions and products or services.

By setting up these internal indices of measurement, an objective evaluation of customer satisfaction can be factored into compensation plans, bonus distributions and promotions. A chart that will be helpful in using internal benchmarking is provided in Figure 13.7.

FIGURE 13.7 Internal Benchmarking Worksheet (continued)

Date:_____   Reviewer: _____

Measurement Dates and Differences (+/−)

Characteristics	Date 1	Date 2	Difference +/−	Date 3	Difference +/−	Date 4	Difference +/−	Date 5	Difference +/−	Date 6	Difference +/−
Courtesy											
Professionalism											
Timeliness											
Product knowledge											
Competence											
Problem-solving skills											
Attitude											
Prices											
Quality											
Selection											
Phone-answering skills											

Scoring: Excellent = 4.0   Good = 3.0   Average = 2.0   Poor = 1.0   Don't know = no score

Special comments/notations: _____

Summary

Benchmarking is an early warning system. It can inform companies of impending problems or identify service opportunities. By using objective measures of performance that are customer oriented and market driven, attention can be focused where it is most needed.

Benchmarking can force companies to recognize their true abilities, performance and shortcomings now, and over a period of time. It encourages companies to move toward change, humility and a greater sense of confidence that they are doing their utmost to provide superior customer service and build customer satisfaction.

Notes on Using the Assessment

The assessment exercise is not intended to be all-inclusive; each organization and the market in which it operates is unique. The questions raised are intended to help an organization go beyond the facade of "rationalizing" its action or inaction. The assessment tools provided herein are intended to be insightful. It is important that each organization determine the specific relevance of the assessment with respect to its specific situation.

Scoring the Assessment

Filling Out the Form

1. If the statement is generally true of your organization, mark the "yes" column.
2. If the statement is not true of your organization, mark the "no" column.
3. If the statement is occasionally true of your organization, mark the "sometimes" column.
4. If a particular statement does not have relevance to your organization or if information is not available for a credible response, then draw a line through the statement.

Evaluating the Responses

1. A negative answer is seldom favorable. It indicates an absence of a particular activity that may or may not be compensated for elsewhere.
2. A positive answer is almost always favorable. However, too many "yes" answers may indicate that your response is not sufficiently objective.
3. Several "sometimes" answers may point to a lack of direction or commitment.
4. Several "crossed off" questions may indicate insufficient records or an inadequate data base.

Rating the Responses

1. Upon completion of the assessment form, award points as follows:
    - For each "yes" answer, award one point.
    - For each "sometimes" answer, award one-half point.
    - For each "no" answer, award zero points.
    - For each question crossed off the list, award zero points, and deduct one from the total number of questions in the assessment.
2. Divide the total number of points awarded by the number of questions on the assessment (less the number of questions crossed off the list).

$$\text{Score} = \frac{\text{Number of points awarded}}{\text{Number of questions answered}}$$

A score of 1 is excellent. Scores less than 1 should be evaluated with respect to their distance from 1. The farther the score is from 1, the more removed the organization is from initiating actions that are beneficial to superior customer service.

Benchmark Assessment

Organization: _____ Date: _____ Person Conducting Assessment: _____

	Yes	No	Sometimes
1. The organization has clearly defined key customer-service characteristics.	_____	_____	_____
2. Management shares these key customer-service characteristics with employees.	_____	_____	_____
3. Management seeks input from employees concerning key customer-service characteristics.	_____	_____	_____
4. The organization measures its performance in key customer-service areas vis-à-vis competitors.	_____	_____	_____
5. The organization studies "premier" organizations that render "top of the class" performance in key customer-service characteristics.	_____	_____	_____
6. The organization measures its internal performance in key customer-service characteristics against previous performance levels.	_____	_____	_____
7. Objective customer input is the foundation upon which benchmarking efforts are based.	_____	_____	_____
8. Improvement in customer satisfaction measurements is a component in each employee's compensation plan.	_____	_____	_____
9. The organization frequently rewards/recognizes employee improvement in serving customers well.	_____	_____	_____

Page total: _____ + _____ + _____ = ⬜

	Yes	No	Sometimes
10. The organization shares the results of benchmark analyses with employees.	————	————	————
11. The organization seeks active employee participation in determining what to measure.	————	————	————
12. Management actively reviews benchmark trends and seeks means of improvement.	————	————	————

Page total: ———— **+** ———— **+** ———— **=** ▢

Page 1 Total: **=** ▢

Page 2 Total: **=** ▢

Exercise Total: **=** ▢

14

Are You Investing Your Resources in the Right Places?

A regionally based accounting firm has grown at a steady rate over a ten-year period. Some of the growth has been fueled by acquiring other firms in the region.

During the ten-year growth period, the managing partner has been proud of the fact that the firm also has added a considerable number of services available to clients.

However, in the last two years, the firm's revenues have been relatively flat. To help assess the situation, the managing partner commissions an assessment of customer satisfaction.

The assessment shows that two-thirds of the services offered are highly regarded and deemed important. However, the clients are not very committed to the remaining one-third.

With such data, the managing partner cuts the other services, cuts the corresponding overhead and reallocates resources to support the preferred services more completely.

The results have been that firm revenues and quarterly profits have increased due to the reduction in overhead and expenses associated with cutting one-third of the services.

It is important for companies to assess their competitive position with respect to other companies in their environment. Such an assessment can help identify strengths and weaknesses vis-à-vis the competition, thereby enabling companies to focus on strengths and eliminate weaknesses.

Few companies can effectively compete against all competitors on all fronts simultaneously. It is important for a firm to identify key strategic points of difference so it can maximize the allocation of finite resources. The key areas to evaluate include markets, customers, products or services offered, personnel, operations/facilities and finances.

To be valuable in the marketplace, companies must maximize the return on available and invested capital. They must regularly evaluate their allocation of resources to different areas. Figure 14.1 is an example of a survey you can use to obtain relevant information from your customers.

Markets

Many companies make decisions about critical components of their operations as if they were in a vacuum, with no sensitivity or awareness of what other companies are doing in the market. To be effective, they should be asking questions such as the following:

- What are the trends in the market?
- In which direction is the market headed?
- What do the customers want versus need?
- Are we aware of the difference?
- What is the size of other competitors in the market?

To have strategic significance, terms or units of measure should be used that enable companies to compare themselves to competitors. Statistics regarding the number of employees or customers a competitor has may have a potential marketing impact. Other information—such as the amount of capital invested, asset base, profits, inventory levels, the number of inventory turns, the number of support personnel and the number of sales representatives—can help determine the investment required to compete effectively and identify areas that may not be well served.

Customers and the Products or Services Offered

Why does a company offer the products or services it offers? Is there a rational process in place by which new products or services are added or deleted from a company's portfolio? Is there a threshold of revenue generation below which a product or service will no longer be carried or offered?

Too often companies offer products or services that management feels *should* be offered; or they continue to offer the products or services they have historically offered, as opposed to what the market dictates. However, companies should periodically assess their offerings and determine whether customers and potential customers are aware of all the products or services in their portfolios. Not long ago a large, well-known law firm disclosed in a meeting that it had budgeted a significant sum toward practice development. Prior to launching the development campaign, the firm performed an assessment on existing clients to determine their awareness of the services offered. Much to their chagrin, the firm found that almost two-thirds of the clients used more than one law firm for their legal work. And upon further analysis through cross-tabulation, the firm found that none of those clients were using other law firms because of dissatisfaction, but rather because they didn't know about the other services the firm provided. Thus, the law firm realized that one of its biggest challenges was to increase the awareness of existing clients before spending significant funds on pursuing new clients.

In another case, a company offered 12 different kinds of services to its customers. Upon careful objective analysis of customer input, it was determined that the customers really only had a viable interest in 7 of the 12 services. At that point, the company had a choice to make: pursue additional customers that may have an interest in the other services or drop the other services and the costs associated with offering them.

The key point in these examples is that by getting good objective information from customers, both organizations were empowered to make decisions that enabled them to allocate resources where they could get the greatest return. Without this information, they would have continued operating in a manner that presumed business as usual and consumed resources in an inefficient manner.

A well-designed customer questionnaire can prove helpful to you in determining the awareness, utilization and interest levels of your customers. A sample customer questionnaire is provided in Figure 14.1.

FIGURE 14.1   Measurement of Customer Awareness, Utilization and Interest in Products or Services

Dear Valued Client,

Our success at XYZ is built around our ability to meet the needs of our clients. Like any business, it is important that we ask ourselves the question, "How are we doing?"

We believe the best approach is to let our clients answer that question for us. By taking a few moments to complete this survey, you will help us evaluate our performance.

We have enclosed a postage-paid envelope for your convenience. To allow for timely processing, please return the questionnaire within seven days of receipt.

We appreciate your willingness to assist us. Thank you for taking the time to respond to our questions. We'll be listening.

Sincerely,

XYZ

Jane Doe
President

Please indicate your company's awareness, utilization (from our company as well as from other companies) and interest. If you have used a particular product or service from our company, please also rate your level of satisfaction with that product or service. Additional space for comments on any or all of our products or services is provided at the bottom of this assessment.

A box that is not checked will be considered a "no" answer.

Products and Services	Aware of product or service	Have used this product or service from this company	Have used this product or service from another company	Interested in this product or service	Rate Our Product/Service Quality (where applicable)		
					High	Medium	Low
Product or service A	❑	❑	❑	❑	H	M	L
Product or service B	❑	❑	❑	❑	H	M	L
Product or service C	❑	❑	❑	❑	H	M	L
And so on . . .	❑	❑	❑	❑	H	M	L

Additional space for comments:

_____

_____

_____

Operations, Facilities and Technology

It is important to periodically assess competitive strategies utilized in the market with respect to operations, facilities and technology. Information concerning competitors in these key areas can provide important insight regarding strategic direction. It is helpful to consider how your competitors compare the following areas:

- Locations of facilities, branch offices, field offices and the types of buildings used
- Creative channels of distribution
- Data bases, communication networks and computers
- Technology downstream with customers, branch offices, field offices, sales representatives, etc.
- Facility management, overall appearance and the integration of other offices or facilities

As many companies must increasingly compete through the allocation of and return on scarce capital, a company's ability to profitably compete will depend on proper deployment and utilization of operational capabilities, facilities management and technology. Customer input is a critically important tool in assessing these areas. A chart that will help you track such developments in the market is provided in Figure 14.2.

The matrix in Figure 14.2 is used most effectively when an objective form of customer assessment is used to produce numerical values or specific valuations for comparative purposes. Spaces have been provided for three competitors, your score and a box in which customer preferences and input are recorded. The number of competitors and components of operations can be selected as appropriate for your organization.

After acquiring this information, you can then proceed through a systematic process of evaluating an efficient allocation of resources. This six-step process is shown in Figures 14.3 and 14.4.

Financial Allocation Decisions

Customer satisfaction information is helpful in allocating the financing and operating responsibilities needed to manage a company. Financ-

FIGURE 14.2   Market Developments Affecting Operations, Facilities and Technology

Organization: _____   Date: _____   Preparer: _____

Competitors	Component of Operations				
	Facilities/ Locations	Creative/ Enhanced Channels of Distribution	Usage of Data Bases, Communication Networks and Computers	Usage of Technology "Downstream" Field Offices, Other Locations, Reps, etc.	Facility Management
1					
2					
3					
Your Organization					
Customer Preference/ Input					

FIGURE 14.3　Six-Step Strategic Assessment of Allocation of Resources

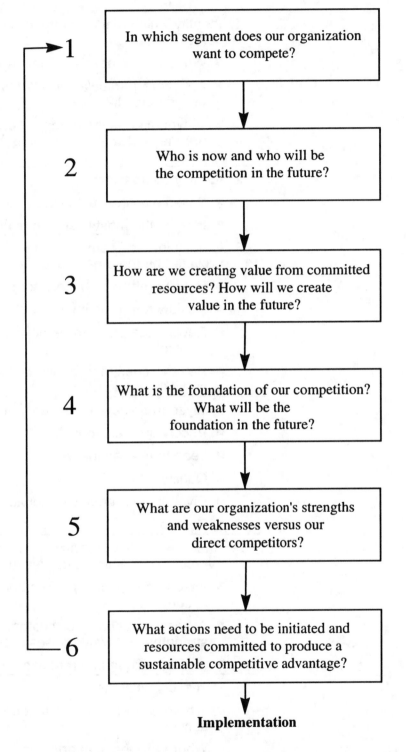

Implementation

Completion of this overall process takes an organization down
the path toward a more accurate strategic allocation of finite
resources while pursuing a strategic advantage in the market.

FIGURE 14.4   Outline of the Six Steps in the Allocation of Resources Assessment

1. Identify which market(s) the organization wants to sell to or serve.
   - What are the needs of the market?
   - Are there particular needs that the organization is uniquely qualified to fill?
   - To whom does the organization presently sell or serve? What are they sold? What about in the future—mid-term and long-term?

2. Identify competitors
   - Select existing customers.
   - Identify the most likely future competition.

3. Identify integral components of the product or service provided by the organization.
   - Review return on assets committed.
   - Review return on investment per customer.
   - Review the process(es) involved in providing the product or service.
   - Review customer relationship—awareness of products or services provided.

4. Analyze the different elements of competition.
   - Price/value relationship.
   - Lead time/availability
   - Quality
   - Diversity of products or services provided
   - Perception

5. Analyze how the organization can build on its strengths and overcome or eliminate its weaknesses.
   - Assess competitor performance vis-à-vis that of the organization.
   - Assess perception of customers with respect to perceived strengths and weaknesses of the organization.
   - Identify unique inherent capabilities of the organization.

6. Derive conclusions.
   - Where are efforts and resources best allocated to achieve success?
   - Where are these efforts and resources presently allocated?

FIGURE 14.5   Return on Total Assets Formula

$$\frac{\text{Net income} + [\text{Interest expense} \times (1-\text{tax rate})]}{\text{Average total assets}} = \text{Return on total assets}$$

Net income		$ 1,500,000
Addition of interest expense $625,000 \times (1 - 0.40)$		$ 375,000
	Total	$ 1,875,000 **(1)**
Assets, beginning of year		$26,720,000
Assets, end of year		$29,000,000
	Total	$55,720,000

Average total assets: $55,720,000 ÷ 2 = $27,860,000 **(2)**

Return on total assets: **(1)** ÷ **(2)** = 6.7%

Note: This calculation can be done by product or service offering, division, office, the entire organization, etc.

---

ing responsibilities pertain to how a company obtains the capital needed to provide for assets. Operating responsibilities relate to how a company uses those assets once they've been obtained.

Return on Total Assets

Another tool that is very helpful in making financial allocation decisions is a calculation on the return on total assets. The return on total assets formula can be used in assessing a product or service, financial performance or an individual customer. It is a measure of how well assets are being utilized—that is, a measure of operating performance. A formula and worksheet for its calculation and analysis are provided in Figures 14.5 and 14.6.

You should view the results of this calculation in the context of customer satisfaction information. If an analysis of return on total assets is not good but the assessment of awareness, utilization and interest shows promise, it may be worth continuing to pursue your objective. However, if the assessment of awareness, utilization and interest proves

---

FIGURE 14.6   Return on Total Assets Worksheet

Date:_____   Product/Service/Organization:_____

Information required:

Net income: _____

Interest expense:_____

Assets, beginning of year:_____

Assets, end of year:_____

Average total assets:_____

$$\frac{\text{Net income} + [\text{Interest expense} \times (1-\text{tax rate})]}{\text{Average total assets}} = \text{Return on total assets}$$

_____ + [_____ × (1– _____)] = Return on total assets

---

disappointing, then your results are further affirmation that your resources can be deployed more effectively elsewhere.

Cost-Benefit Analysis

Another financial measurement, called the *cost-benefit analysis*, can prove helpful in allocating your company's financial resources. By carefully measuring specific levels of customer satisfaction on a product-by-product or service-by-service basis, your company can then know how each element is faring from the customer's perspective.

Break-Even Analysis

A tool that helps assess the continuance of a product or service is the break-even analysis. Simply defined, the *break-even point* occurs where total sales revenue equals total expenses (variable and fixed). Break-even analysis helps a company determine whether to go forward in launching a new product or service or to continue offering an existing product or service.

The calculated break-even point, as illustrated in Figure 14.7, determines how many units (products, services, engagements, memberships, patients, clients, etc.) must be successfully engaged for a company to at

FIGURE 14.7   Break-Even Formula

Sales = Variable expenses + Fixed expenses + Profit

At the break-even point, profits will be zero. Thus, the break-even point can be calculated by finding the point where sales just equal the total of the variable expenses plus the fixed expenses.

Example:
Sales = Variable expenses + Fixed expenses + Profit
$$\$250x = \$150x + \$35,000 + 0$$
$$100x = \$35,000$$
$$x = 350 \text{ units}$$

where:
x = break-even point in particular product or service units.
$250 = unit price
$150 = unit variable expenses
$35,000 = total fixed expenses

Note: This calculation can be done by product or service offering, division, office, the entire organization, etc.

least cover its costs. While reviewing the numbers derived from a break-even analysis to assess the reasonableness and/or probability of attaining a particular level, a company can factor in valuable customer-based information gleaned from an assessment of awareness, utilization and interest to aid in the process of determining if such levels are also realistic in light of customer satisfaction. Figure 14.8 provides a basis format to use in assessing individual products or services in your organization.

FIGURE 14.8   Break-Even Analysis Worksheet

Date:_____   Product/Service/Organization:_____

Information required:

Unit sales price: _____

Unit variable expenses: _____

Total fixed expenses: _____

Sales = variable expenses + fixed expenses + profits

_____ = _____ + _____ + __0__

Notes on Using the Assessment

The assessment exercise is not intended to be all-inclusive; each organization and the market in which it operates is unique. The questions raised are intended to help an organization go beyond the facade of "rationalizing" its action or inaction. The assessment tools provided herein are intended to be insightful. It is important that each organization determine the specific relevance of the assessment with respect to its specific situation.

Scoring the Assessment

Filling Out the Form

1. If the statement is generally true of your organization, mark the "yes" column.
2. If the statement is not true of your organization, mark the "no" column.
3. If the statement is occasionally true of your organization, mark the "sometimes" column.
4. If a particular statement does not have relevance to your organization or if information is not available for a credible response, then draw a line through the statement.

Evaluating the Responses

1. A negative answer is seldom favorable. It indicates an absence of a particular activity that may or may not be compensated for elsewhere.
2. A positive answer is almost always favorable. However, too many "yes" answers may indicate that your response is not sufficiently objective.
3. Several "sometimes" answers may point to a lack of direction or commitment.
4. Several "crossed off" questions may indicate insufficient records or an inadequate data base.

Rating the Responses

1. Upon completion of the assessment form, award points as follows:
   - For each "yes" answer, award one point.
   - For each "sometimes" answer, award one-half point.
   - For each "no" answer, award zero points.
   - For each question crossed off the list, award zero points, and deduct one from the total number of questions in the assessment.
2. Divide the total number of points awarded by the number of questions on the assessment (less the number of questions crossed off the list).

$$\text{Score} = \frac{\text{Number of points awarded}}{\text{Number of questions answered}}$$

A score of 1 is excellent. Scores less than 1 should be evaluated with respect to their distance from 1. The farther the score is from 1, the more removed the organization is from initiating actions that are beneficial to superior customer service.

Allocation of Resources Assessment

Organization: _____ Date: _____ Person Conducting Assessment: _____

	Yes	No	Sometimes
1. The organization periodically assesses interest, utilization and awareness levels of its products and/or services.	_____	_____	_____
2. The organization establishes threshold levels of revenue or profit a product or service must generate to be kept in its portfolio.	_____	_____	_____
3. The organization periodically assesses products or services customers want.	_____	_____	_____
4. The organization regularly assesses competitive strategies regarding resource allocation.	_____	_____	_____
5. Changes in the competitive environment are monitored throughout the new product or new service development process so changes in timing and direction can be made as needed.	_____	_____	_____
6. Consistent use of strategic competitive analysis is made by management in assessing viability of products and services.	_____	_____	_____
7. Review of resource allocation is specifically assigned on the organizational chart and is carefully monitored.	_____	_____	_____
8. The organization has a specific budget allocation for strategic competitive assessment of resource allocation.	_____	_____	_____

Page total: _____ + _____ + _____ = ☐

	Yes	No	Sometimes
9. Competitive evaluations regularly and promptly detect significant competitive developments with respect to resource allocation strategies.	——	——	——
10. The effectiveness of resource allocation reviews is periodically measured and evaluated.	——	——	——
11. The organization actively participates in seeking key industry information that illustrates important industry trends with respect to resource allocation.	——	——	——
12. Management actively seeks input with respect to maximizing the return on invested capital.	——	——	——

Page total: —— + —— + —— = ☐

Page 1 Total: = ☐

Page 2 Total: = ☐

Exercise Total: = ☐

15 Planning Your Future

Although they compete in one of the most cyclical industries anywhere, Alex and his associates always seem to be well organized, in control and leaders in sales and profitability.

When asked to explain his relative calmness and that of his associates, Alex responds that it is because of an incessant commitment to planning the firm's direction—where it has been and where it wants to go—within the context of the dynamics of the marketplace.

One executive has said, "In the past I did not take the time as skipper of this ship to plot our course. The absence of direction created a vacuum where improvising rushed in. The resulting chaos and hodgepodge forced me to recognize that I must take the time to think through where we want to go."

Planning for the future requires a thorough and realistic understanding of existing products, services, markets, margins, profits, return on allocated capital, availability of capital, innovation and the availability and skills of employees. When contemplating a company's specific mission, management must have a clear understanding of how well the company is doing today. As has been demonstrated throughout this book, customer input and assessment of satisfaction can play an enormously important role in setting objectives.

Prudent Planning

Prudent planning is designed to help a company, regardless of its size, focus on where it wants to be three to five years into the future. Too often managers are totally focused on short-term needs and prospects, largely because of their immediacy. Consequently, long-term problems and opportunities are deferred or given only brief attention. It is important for management to distinguish between current operating challenges and longer-term goals and plans.

Some executives search for ways to increase the size, efficiency and profitability of their operations. But, if the forecasted performance of existing operations fails to produce expectations of profitable growth, many of them build upon the operations that presently exist and accept the status quo.

Strategic Planning

There are some executives who are not satisfied with nominal growth rates into the future. Empowered with well-founded, customer-based information (e.g., satisfaction measurements; awareness and utilization of product and service information; and customer wants, needs, expectations, perceived strengths and weaknesses and suggestions for improvement), they stretch the forecasts and establish new and challenging standards of performance for the future.

Thus, an increasing number of companies are realizing the importance of strategic planning. Several large companies go to the extreme of considering a range of plans that cover simultaneous possibilities across a wide set of assumptions. However, this involved approach usually requires a highly structured strategic planning process and a large planning staff.

Although this type of intensive approach has considerable benefits, few companies can afford such a commitment. Smaller companies or larger companies without extensive strategic planning resources can use a simplified approach more effectively. The underlying assumption with this approach is that a person or group can only commit part-time efforts to the strategic planning process. This ten-step process is graphically represented in Figure 15.1. A more detailed version of the process is as follows:

Step 1: Identify and clarify the company's mission, objectives and policies.

Mission: What is your company's basic purpose? Because of existing strengths and prior commitments, you may not be able to change your mission for a few years (unless core assumptions have been shaken by customer input, which would necessitate a drastic change).

Basic objectives: Does your company have long-term objectives, such as size, market share, profitability, sales level, etc? If minimum future standards have not been set, what are your common sense minimums?

Policies: Are there certain limitations placed on the company? If so, they should be clearly delineated.

Step 2: Determine how far into the future you want the strategic plan to extend. Most strategic plans are for a three- to five-year period. Remember that strategic planning will give your company an enhanced understanding of the possible variations in future markets and subsequently, the long-range consequences of today's decisions.

Step 3: Derive a thorough understanding of your company's strengths and weaknesses vis-à-vis the market. Look at your company's market segment. What was it like 5, 10 or 20 years ago versus today. What caused the changes? Then review the company over the same time spans. What are the similarities and differences between your company and the market segment in which it competes?

Step 4: Identify factors that you think will definitely take place within the strategic planning time frame. Your assumptions should be as accurate and conclusive as possible.

Step 5: List key variables that could have critical consequences for your company. Remember to include the variables that have been crucial to your company in the past as well as those that will be important in the future. The variables used should be easily predicted and measured. (For simplicity, limit them to four or five.)

Step 6: Give reasonable values to each key variable. To maintain objectivity, seek the input of other objectives, staff, others within the industry and, if possible, customers and suppliers.

Step 7: Develop three or four scenarios in which the company could operate in a specified time frame. It is important to keep the scenarios plausible.

Step 8: Derive a strategy for each scenario that would most likely result in reaching your objectives.

Step 9: Check the flexibility of each strategy by testing its effectiveness within other scenarios.

Step 10: Develop an ideal response strategy. Such a strategy should have the following characteristics:

- It should provide maximum adaptability.
- It should produce favorable outcomes in scenarios with a relatively high likelihood of occurrence.
- It should be relatively attractive in the near term, since the long term is less predictable.

Always keep in mind that a sound reliance on objective, customer-based information; a commitment to providing superior customer service; and a strong dose of common sense should permeate the entire ten-step planning process.

FIGURE 15.1   Ten Steps for Business Strategic Planning

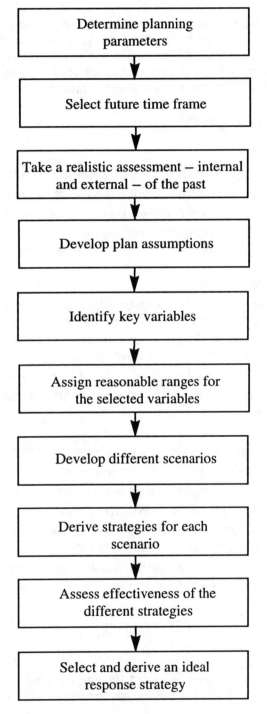

Note: Objectively obtained customer-based data plays a critical role in each step of the process. Strategic planning will be seriously flawed if it does not draw extensively upon customer satisfaction data when looking at an organization historically and planning for it prospectively.

Notes on Using the Assessment

The assessment exercise is not intended to be all-inclusive; each organization and the market in which it operates is unique. The questions raised are intended to help an organization go beyond the facade of "rationalizing" its action or inaction. The assessment tools provided herein are intended to be insightful. It is important that each organization determine the specific relevance of the assessment with respect to its specific situation.

Scoring the Assessment

Filling Out the Form

1. If the statement is generally true of your organization, mark the "yes" column.
2. If the statement is not true of your organization, mark the "no" column.
3. If the statement is occasionally true of your organization, mark the "sometimes" column.
4. If a particular statement does not have relevance to your organization or if information is not available for a credible response, then draw a line through the statement.

Evaluating the Responses

1. A negative answer is seldom favorable. It indicates an absence of a particular activity that may or may not be compensated for elsewhere.
2. A positive answer is almost always favorable. However, too many "yes" answers may indicate that your response is not sufficiently objective.
3. Several "sometimes" answers may point to a lack of direction or commitment.
4. Several "crossed off" questions may indicate insufficient records or an inadequate data base.

Rating the Responses

1. Upon completion of the assessment form, award points as follows:
   - For each "yes" answer, award one point.
   - For each "sometimes" answer, award one-half point.
   - For each "no" answer, award zero points.
   - For each question crossed off the list, award zero points, and deduct one from the total number of questions in the assessment.
2. Divide the total number of points awarded by the number of questions on the assessment (less the number of questions crossed off the list).

$$\text{Score} = \frac{\text{Number of points awarded}}{\text{Number of questions answered}}$$

A score of 1 is excellent. Scores less than 1 should be evaluated with respect to their distance from 1. The farther the score is from 1, the more removed the organization is from initiating actions that are beneficial to superior customer service.

Strategic Planning Assessment

Organization: _____ Date: _____ Person Conducting Assessment: _____

	Yes	No	Sometimes
1. The organization regularly collects market information for future comparative purposes.	_____	_____	_____
2. The organization has a clearly defined mission.	_____	_____	_____
3. If defined, the mission is shared with employees for affirmation and input.	_____	_____	_____
4. The organization has an ongoing prudent planning process.	_____	_____	_____
5. The organization collects and uses objective customer-based information as an integral part of its prudent planning process.	_____	_____	_____
6. Management has a strong commitment to the prudent planning process.	_____	_____	_____
7. The organization has clearly defined long-term objectives.	_____	_____	_____
8. The organization regularly assesses its strengths and weaknesses vis-à-vis the market.	_____	_____	_____
9. The organization regularly assesses its position in the market from a historical perspective and also assesses possible ramifications for the future.	_____	_____	_____
10. The organization has a clear understanding of where it wants to go in three to five years.	_____	_____	_____

Page total: _____ + _____ + _____ = ☐

	Yes	No	Sometimes
11. The organization has a strong commitment to improving customer service as a component of its strategic plan.	————	————	————
12. The organization regularly checks assumptions upon which key variable allocations are made.	————	————	————

Page total: ———— + ———— + ———— = ☐

Page 1 Total: = ☐

Page 2 Total: = ☐

Exercise Total: = ☐

16

The Internet: Modern Electronic Communication

The president of a small computer company in the Southeast has long considered establishing a Web site for his firm. He has heard stories of how it has transformed many companies into overnight successes. Fearing that time is slipping away and with it his chance for a competitive advantage, the executive moves quickly to have a Web site created for his firm.

After several months have passed, his firm's revenues have not increased as he had hoped. In fact, revenues have actually declined in most months compared to the prior year's performance. One day, one of his most reliable customers calls and shares considerable frustration about his firm and suggests that as a result he is considering taking his business elsewhere. Greatly concerned, as well as puzzled, by his friend's remarks, the executive asks his friend to share in detail the areas in which he has experienced problems.

The friend explains that he has had difficulty on numerous occasions with the company's Web site in terms of accessing information, ordering, follow-up and the amount of time it took to access various windows. The customer concludes with the overview statement that he has to work too hard to do business with the company.

Steadily lower information processing costs and increasing computational capabilities frequently require significant changes in the way businesses compete for and retain customers. Technological innovations have made it realistic to create customer feedback loops at an individual level like never before. As a result, customers and businesses together can define commercial expectations in an interactive and collaborative environment. Increasingly, the dynamics of contemporary competition are at the individual level—one customer at a time.

Technological modifications such as the World Wide Web and the Internet provide significant potential in terms of how your company works in identifying and meeting customer wants, needs and expectations. The Web has opened up a new and different type of customer dialogue. It has introduced the plausibility of an automated conversation between customer and product/service provider. It provides a forum in which customers can be known as individuals and treated as such. Expectations are moving steadily towards "immediacy." Everything is expected instantly—everything is faster. Integrating the customer into the mix of an environment of such immediacy can be a distinctive competitive advantage—and, if absent from your company, a distinctive disadvantage.

It would be unfortunate if companies were not to utilize new means of effectively communicating with their customers. However, in many instances, that is exactly what is happening with the Internet. Many companies build World Wide Web sites to communicate *to* their customers instead of *with* them. Most Web sites to date have been created as electronic brochures—online television ads, or an Internet version of a sales pitch. Such a forum often enables people to get the information they are interested in, but little thought or planning is given to the two-way communication capability available. It is a missed opportunity of considerable significance.

The Internet offers a new means in which to establish a rapport with customers. Solving customer problems, answering customer questions, and selling them additional products and services can all be computerized. The Web can also be a useful tool in measuring and managing customer satisfaction and helping to solidify the relationship between buyer and seller.

A well thought out and well constructed Web site can provide numerous benefits. It can provide the information customers want, when they want it, and in as much or as little detail as desired. Customers can answer their own questions, at a time of their own choosing, and at a level of their preference. Such benefits can yield financial savings in having fewer people to answer the phone in that respective area, and savings on brochures being printed, stored, picked, packed and mailed. However, some of the greatest benefits may be in higher levels of customer satisfaction from giving customers ready access to information and problem resolution in sufficient detail and minimum time.

The challenge is to create a Web site that is useful and meaningful to your organization and your existing and prospective customers. From such a starting point, your company will no doubt move up the value chain as your customers demand more. This electronic forum, while providing considerable benefits to your existing and prospective customers, can also provide your company with an unparalleled amount of information concerning your customers, as they disclose their wants, needs and expectations, their likes and dislikes, their perceptions of your organizational strengths and weaknesses, and suggestions for improvement.

Nonstop 24-Hour World Wide Web World

One of the more important reasons for Web-based customer service is the feasibility of offering full-time availability. Customers are becoming increasingly sophisticated and are expecting better and better service. Customer service from 9:00 to 5:00 is usually not enough in many customers' minds. Customers are expecting greater access to product information, order status detail and other specific account information on a timely basis (e.g., available discount levels, aggregate orders, remaining credit line available, product availability, current credit aging, delivery schedule, sales rep information, etc.).

Customer Perspective

As has been referenced throughout this book, customer satisfaction and successful customer service means always looking at your company, your policies, and your products and services from your customers' perspective. The customer probably doesn't care very much if your company is organized by product line, business unit, division or geographical orientation. Simply put, the customer wants her question answered, need fulfilled or problem solved.

One of the more important tasks for a customer service Web builder is to understand what the customer wants to see, wants to ask and wants to get from the experience. It may prove helpful to directly ask existing and prospective customers who do business with you via a Web site about what sort of functionality they would like to see. Ideally, a function of one of the components of the Web site would regularly ask customers about their experience. Care must be taken to provide customers ample opportunity to click on buttons that let you know about different aspects of their experience with your company (and its Web site); for example, how they rate the service, competitive assessments, areas for improvement, etc. Numerous opportunities should be provided for customers to augment automated responses with written opinions.

Elements To Consider

Frequently Asked Questions (FAQ) Page

This is an initial step and a document that is frequently expected in better Web sites. The FAQ is a place of introduction that provides basic site fundamentals and allows seekers from the casually curious to the more sophisticated to get up to speed as quickly as possible.

Determining which questions to include in a company's FAQ should be relatively straightforward. Your company's customer service people (e.g., those manning the 800 number, those making service calls and frontline salespeople) can probably provide a good overview of frequently asked questions. You may want to consider having two FAQ pages: one for relatively new and prospective customers with more basic questions, and one for existing customers who have greater familiarity with your products and services.

The organization of an FAQ page requires serious planning. Well-organized FAQs will be accessed often and will save your company and customers a significant amount of phone time. The FAQ should be easy to find on the site and easy to read. The page should be easy to navigate and expectations must be managed so that browsers do not spend time looking only to be disappointed.

Search Capability

The first time that somebody comes to your Web site they are probably going to look around, see what is there and possibly review the FAQ page. Subsequent visits will probably be driven by specific need. Either your Web site helps them find what they want quickly or they may stop thinking of your Web site as a resource. For customer ease of use, an effective and efficient search tool should be readily accessible from the home page and also from any page on the site. It is important that the scope and capability of the search tool mechanism fit the site appropriately. The size and depth of your Web site should determine the searching capability needed for effective and efficient use by your customers. However, it is important to keep the customer's needs and ease of use in mind.

Managing Expectations

It is best to be clear about what is available on your Web site and what is not. Customers frequently wonder how difficult it will be to interact with and how long it will take to find the information they are seeking. It is important to be as straightforward and helpful as possible as early in the process as is feasible.

For example, even with FAQs to review and databases to scan, even the most sophisticated customers may not be able to solve a problem— even one that has been addressed before and is described clearly in the FAQ. Running into a series of dead ends does not help build customer confidence in the company or service provided. Sometimes a well trained customer service person is needed to ask the customer the proper questions in the appropriate context.

To help monitor such a need, a company should consider utilizing a search tool gauge that can help track the number of searches an individual makes. If a certain customer exceeds averages for your company's Web site, your company could deliver an offer of special assistance through e-mail, fax, or phone.

E-mail

E-mail provides an efficient and seamless way to communicate. It has been said that e-mail is the glue that cements the Internet together. It is important to acknowledge that e-mail is the voice of your customer. The rest of your company's Web site is, for the most part, from the perspective of inside out—trying to give customers what they need. E-mail is from the perspective of the outside coming in and requires diligent care.

By providing your customer service department with e-mail capability, you give your customers one more means to communicate with your company. However, employees must understand that responding to a customer comment, question or complaint via e-mail demands the same care and diligence used when responding over the phone and in writing. Over the phone, voice inflection and perceived attitudes and demeanor are very important in nurturing a vital customer/seller relationship. The "right" answer given or spoken in the wrong way can have a negative effect. The wrong written words can hurt even the most the well-intentioned customer service representative. The casual nature of e-mail can be misleading.

It is advisable that a company policy for using e-mail be created. Clarity and professionalism should be emphasized. (See Chapter 12 for suggestions concerning written correspondence.) Another significant component of the policy should be the overall directing and managing of received e-mail. Lost or "stale" e-mail messages do little to imply quality or professionalism on the part of your company from the perspective of the customer. To bring about an efficient and professional method of directing the receipt of and answering of e-mail, a method of segmentation with triage characteristics is helpful. For example, incoming e-mail could be assigned to one of six primary categories:

1. Customer service (including refunds, returns, order tracking, product suggestions or complaints)

2. Accounting (including accounts receivable/payable)

3. Sales (including product/service availability, product information, terms, discounts)

4. Human resources (including references, resumes, proof of employment, interview requests, job openings)

5. Public relations (including community affairs, journalistic inquiries, sponsorships)

6. Other (including areas not listed above)

Ideally, one person is assigned responsibility for the particular area and reviews incoming e-mail in a triagelike manner with each classification having a standard of responsiveness. The triage classifications could be as follows:

- *Level 1:* A suggestion received requiring basic follow-up, e.g., a thank you
- *Level 2:* Standard inquiry; standard response time required (e.g., 24 hours)
- *Level 3:* Growing problem—referred to appropriate department and corresponding action required
- *Level 4:* Critical situation—management alerted for immediate attention.
- *Level 5:* Battle conditions—all available personnel alerted and pressed into service

This type of segmentation helps allocate resources to where they are most needed while not running the risk of any incoming e-mail messages falling through the cracks. Predetermined policies and procedures can help nurture the customer/company relationship in terms of the timeliness and appropriateness of the response.

Proactive E-mail

The effective use of e-mail within the context of customer satisfaction and customer service is more than waiting for people to complain, seek problem resolution or request information on products and services. E-mail provides a means by which your company can service its customers even before they ask by periodically inquiring as to the status of the relationship from their perspective. Two techniques are very effective in implementing such an approach.

1. Newsletter via e-mail. For the most part, people appreciate being kept up to date by receiving summaries of industry developments, product promotions, helpful suggestions and insightful case studies on how your products and services can be used more effectively. E-mail is a great forum for disseminating such information. However, care must be taken to obtain customer permission to send such material via e-mail. With permission granted, a well-written e-mail newsletter is an excellent tool to enhance customer satisfaction.

2. Electronic surveys. In addition to disseminating a company newsletter, e-mail can also serve as an effective vehicle by which to survey your customers in a periodic or ongoing manner. However, as discussed in Chapters 5 and 6 respectively, great care must be employed to assure compliance with sound statistical methodology. Automation of poor technique will only hasten the acquisition of invalid data.

High-Tech/High-Touch

Although e-mail and the Internet provide a wonderful means of disseminating and collecting information, it is important not to lose sight of the high-tech/high-touch continuum. In 1982, *Megatrends* author John Naisbitt found that people desire increasing personal attention as things become more automated. Naisbitt's findings were more than 15 years ago—a time considerably less automated than today. Although many people may find and use your Web site to get information and solve problems, and your company may have made a considerable effort in time and resources to automate customer service, some may be unable to figure out how to use it, may not be able to find an answer, or may be intimidated by the high-tech interface. When this happens, it is very important that they can readily find a person that can help them.

Caveats

For many companies, the Internet is a technology in search of a strategy. Companies need to have a strategic framework that can traverse the gap between just connecting to the Internet and using its power to competitive advantage. The most beneficial applications on the Internet are those that allow companies to overcome barriers to communication and create connections that serve to improve customer satisfaction and productivity and stimulate development. Technology in and of itself does not create change—people do. Nor does a sophisticated technical infrastructure generate revenue on its own—customers do.

As companies look to participate in cyberspace technology the customer must remain the focus. By focusing on the customer, a company seeking to participate in electronic commerce will see to it that an appropriate infrastructure is in place that facilitates customer interface; not the least of which is a sensitivity to accurate financial interchange and maintenance of customer privacy.

This new and evolving electronic medium is an exciting and dynamic forum, a forum that with proper planning and implementation can be a significant addition to a company's tool kit in measuring and managing customer satisfaction.

Notes on Using the Assessment

The assessment exercise is not intended to be all-inclusive; each organization and the market in which it operates is unique. The questions raised are intended to help an organization go beyond the facade of "rationalizing" its action or inaction. The assessment tools provided herein are intended to be insightful. It is important that each organization determine the specific relevance of the assessment with respect to its specific situation.

Scoring the Assessment

Filling Out the Form

1. If the statement is generally true of your organization, mark the "yes" column.
2. If the statement is not true of your organization, mark the "no" column.
3. If the statement is occasionally true of your organization, mark the "sometimes" column.
4. If a particular statement does not have relevance to your organization or if information is not available for a credible response, then draw a line through the statement.

Evaluating the Responses

1. A negative answer is seldom favorable. It indicates an absence of a particular activity that may or may not be compensated for elsewhere.
2. A positive answer is almost always favorable. However, too many "yes" answers may indicate that your response is not sufficiently objective.
3. Several "sometimes" answers may point to a lack of direction or commitment.
4. Several "crossed off" questions may indicate insufficient records or an inadequate data base.

Rating the Responses

1. Upon completion of the assessment form, award points as follows:
    - For each "yes" answer, award one point.
    - For each "sometimes" answer, award one-half point.
    - For each "no" answer, award zero points.
    - For each question crossed off the list, award zero points, and deduct one from the total number of questions in the assessment.
2. Divide the total number of points awarded by the number of questions on the assessment (less the number of questions crossed off the list).

$$\text{Score} = \frac{\text{Number of points awarded}}{\text{Number of questions answered}}$$

A score of 1 is excellent. Scores less than 1 should be evaluated with respect to their distance from 1. The farther the score is from 1, the more removed the organization is from initiating actions that are beneficial to superior customer service.

Internet Assessment

Organization: _____ Date: _____ Person Conducting Assessment: _____

	Yes	No	Sometimes
1. The organization includes customer service personnel in the preparation of FAQ pages.	_____	_____	_____
2. The company Web site is designed with the customer in mind.	_____	_____	_____
3. Customers are asked to assess, with some frequency, the various aspects of interfacing with the company via the Web site.	_____	_____	_____
4. Personnel are available to aid customers in the event that difficulties are encountered on the company's Web site.	_____	_____	_____
5. A tracking gauge is inherent within the Web site to identify customers encountering disproportionate levels of difficulty so that the company can offer assistance.	_____	_____	_____
6. The company uses e-mail to communicate with customers via an electronic newsletter.	_____	_____	_____
7. When the company sends an e-mail newsletter it obtains customer permission to do so.	_____	_____	_____
8. The company uses e-mail to survey customers.	_____	_____	_____
9. E-mail surveys are designed in strict adherence to sound statistical methodology.	_____	_____	_____

Page total: _____ + _____ + _____ = ☐

	Yes	No	Sometimes
10. Incoming e-mail is managed by specific people who allocate it to various segments in a triagelike manner with requisite performance standards.	——	——	——
11. Company has a developed policy outlining appropriate e-mail formats and protocol.	——	——	——
12. Company has staff training in place to facilitate internal usage of Internet capabilities.	——	——	——
13. The company Web site is designed with an adequate search capability.	——	——	——
14. The company routinely checks its Web site for ease of access and customer friendliness.	——	——	——

Page total: —— + —— + —— = ☐

Page 1 Total: = ☐

Page 2 Total: = ☐

Exercise Total: = ☐

Epilogue:
A Call to Action

A management consultant recently wrote, "Future historians may well describe the 1980s and possibly the 1990s as the era of customer sovereignty. Perhaps 'customer rebellion' is more accurate." To a large extent, which organizations will prosper in today's economy will depend on which organizations recognize the "customer rebellion" and make the necessary preparations to provide superior customer service.

Now is the time for every organization to vigorously assess the status and quality of its relationships with its external customers (existing, potential and past) and with its internal customers (employees). Where do we stand? What do we need to improve? How can we improve? Remember the following points:

- Customers, potential customers and former customers perceive value in their own terms. If your organization wants to meet their needs, you must always look at your products and services from *their* prospective.

- Customers, potential customers and former customers think that your organization's reason for being in business is to meet their needs.

- If your organization sincerely desires to deal successfully with dissatisfied customers, employees must be empowered to focus on saving the customer, not the sale.

- Organizations should strive to provide a dissatisfied customer with a positive reason for dealing with them again.

- In all likelihood, an organization's employees will not treat customers or potential customers any better than they are treated by the organization itself.

- Input from customers, potential customers, or past customers is very valuable. An organization should actively seek, appreciate and review the input.

- The entire process by which an organization creates and delivers its products and services should exhibit superior customer service and support the creation of high levels of customer satisfaction.

Regardless of the size of an organization, it is increasingly difficult to compete primarily on the basis of price or product. In many cases product differentiation is imperceptible. Thus, in the burgeoning battle for the customer, the key is usually not product superiority (at least not for long) but service. The quality of service provided has rapidly become the standard by which organizations are definitively judged. Thus, customer satisfaction and its continual improvement has become a primary indication of sustainability.

In a world of increasing complexity and automation, the successful organization must find the means by which it can operate efficiently and profitably while maintaining a commitment to manage with integrity, compassion, intelligence, competitiveness and an unwavering commitment to providing superior customer service and generating high levels of customer satisfaction.

Although not on the balance sheet, customers are the greatest asset that any organization has. They need to be treated as treasured, long-term investments that, if properly nurtured and cultivated, will provide significant dividends.

How do you know how you're doing with your customers, your prospective customers and employees? Are they satisfied? Do they perceive that you have a strong commitment to providing superior service? The only way to know for certain is to ask—candidly, objectively and with good methodology. As Yogi Berra said so well, "The only way to begin is to begin."

Regardless of the type of organization or size, I encourage you to seize the competitive advantage, provide superior customer service and build high levels of customer satisfaction. Keep up the good fight!

Index

How to Maximize Organizational Performance

Arthur Andersen's Business Consulting practice assists mid- and large-sized companies in improving their business processes and technologies through operational and organizational improvement, performance measurement and middle market technology implementation services. Arthur Andersen can help you:

- ✏ Move your company to a customer driven culture.
- ✏ Achieve seamless customer contact through creative application of technology.
- ✏ Understand and satisfy your customers.
- ✏ Develop a channel strategy to improve service and efficiency.
- ✏ Understand which customers are high value customers.
- ✏ Design programs to retain profitable customers.
- ✏ Develop performance measures that support your corporate strategy.

For more information, please contact

Michael J. Wing, Houston
Phone: 713-237-5043
Fax: 713-373-0894
E-mail: michael.j.wing@ArthurAndersen.com

Joseph P. O'Leary, Chicago
Phone: 312-507-4160
Fax: 312-507-6748
E-mail: joseph.p.o'leary@ArthurAndersen.com

Howard C. Barrett, London
Phone: 44 171 438 5369
Fax: 44 171 831 1133
E-mail: howard.c.barrett@ArthurAndersen.com

Arthur Andersen is a multidisciplinary professional services firm that provides client service through economic and financial consulting, business consulting, tax and business advisory services, and audit and business advisory services. Its professionals combine extensive technical competence and industry experience with innovative and progressive thought to assist clients in improving business performance. Arthur Andersen is a business unit of Andersen Worldwide, the world's largest professional services provider, with more than 91,000 personnel in 79 countries. Its global practice is conducted by member firms in 381 locations.

Customer Satisfaction Does Not Ensure Profitability, Finds Arthur Andersen Study

Study Finds "Missing Links" In Many Customer Satisfaction Programs

A single-minded focus on customer satisfaction does not guarantee profitability, reports an Arthur Andersen study on the best practices in customer satisfaction. Instead, the study finds that corporations must recognize the "missing links" in their current strategies and then align customer satisfaction initiatives with corporate focus, market understanding, value sharing, and process alignment.

"Many corporations erroneously believe that there is a direct correlation between customer satisfaction and the bottom line. This is a dangerously false premise in an age when deregulation and competitive necessity are forcing numerous industries to rethink the way they operate and satisfy their customers," says Joe O'Leary, partner in Arthur Andersen's Business Consulting Practice, who led the customer satisfaction study.

The study found that companies must look beyond customer satisfaction surveys and integrate customer satisfaction practices at all levels. The companies that do this effectively gain an intimate understanding of customers, motivate employees to "own" customers' problems and discover new and better ways to align processes to customer needs. Specific best practices include the following:

- *"Stretch" your management.* Leaders must incorporate customer satisfaction and financial aspirations into their overall corporate objectives. Some leaders set "stretch" goals that are so ambitious they force people in the company to completely rethink the way they conduct business.
- *Walk a mile in your customer's shoes.* Companies must better motivate employees of all levels to understand the needs and wants of their market so that they can better meet their customer's needs.
- *Improve communication.* Companies must encourage interaction and face-to-face meetings between employees and customers, as well as prepare and motivate employees to "own" a customer's problem.
- *Listen, listen, listen.* When developing new services or realigning processes, ask the customer for his/her advice.

For a copy of the executive summary of this study, please contact Joseph P. O'Leary or Howard C. Barrett.

Joseph P. O'Leary, Chicago
Phone: 312-507-4160
Fax: 312-507-6748
E-mail: joseph.p.o'leary@ArthurAndersen.com

Howard C. Barrett, London
Phone: 44 171 438 5369
Fax: 44 171 831 1133
E-mail: howard.c.barrett@ArthurAndersen.com

FOR INSIGHT INTO GREATER CUSTOMER SATISFACTION, A HOSPITAL CHECKED INTO THE HOTEL INDUSTRY.

WHERE SHOULD YOU CHECK IN?

Check out your own creative insights with the help of the Global Best Practices℠ approach. Arthur Andersen professionals will then work closely with you to implement effective solutions.

Their secret? Years of five-star experience. Plus, the unequaled Global Best Practices knowledge base, reserved exclusively for Arthur Andersen. It's the first of its kind and still without peer.

Continuously enriched, it abounds with breakthrough *quantitative* tools along with *qualitative* best practices compiled from worldwide client experience and exhaustive research. Plus, published examples like the hospital that patterned its service after that of a world-class hotel's.

Find out how Arthur Andersen can help your company deliver greater customer satisfaction. Call Vicki Hitzhusen at (713) 237-5113.

GLOBAL BEST PRACTICES℠
PUTTING INSIGHT INTO PRACTICE.℠

ARTHUR ANDERSEN & CO, SC